Praise for *Clay*

"You know you're in for a wild ride when a book drops you into the Body Farm on the first page. From investigations of charred corpses to intensive work on boxes of unidentified skulls, *Clay and Bones* is a gripping account of the day-to-day duties of an FBI forensic artist. And if you think reconstructing someone's face from decades-old remains is Bailey's most difficult challenge, you're in for a big surprise."

—**Lindsey Fitzharris**, author of *The Facemaker*

"After performing thousands of autopsies and writing dozens of articles and three books on the subject of messy death, the two of us learned things from Lisa Bailey. *Clay and Bones* surprises even us, and that's really saying something!"

—**Judy Melinek, MD**, and **T.J. Mitchell**, authors of *Working Stiff*

"A fascinating account! Lisa Bailey deserves both our deepest respect and our profound admiration. I say this, first, in tribute to her incisive intellect, as revealed in these astonishing pages, that led to groundbreaking work in forensic investigation. And, just as important, I say this in honor of her unflinching courage in the face of the flagrant gender discrimination and despicable administrative dishonesty she was forced to endure in her FBI workplace. The bureau prides itself on being one of the world's top law enforcement agencies, but the lack of any sense of internal justice within the ranks of its upper management reveals an organization that has much to answer for."

—**Douglas Schofield**, coauthor of *Giovanni's Ring*

"Lisa Bailey's story covering her fascinating career as a forensic artist and the bizarre treatment she endured while employed at the FBI is as compelling as a crime novel. In *Clay and Bones*, readers have a front-row seat to the real world of forensic art and the real fight for justice Ms. Bailey braved for years at the very agency that claims justice as the primary goal."

—**Melissa Ross**, author of *Forensics for Kids*

CLAY AND BONES

My Life as an
FBI Forensic Artist

LISA BAILEY

First hardcover edition published in 2024
First paperback edition published in 2025
Published by Chicago Review Press Incorporated
814 North Franklin Street
Chicago, Illinois 60610
ISBN 978-0-89733-444-0

The Library of Congress has cataloged the hardcover edition
under the following Control Number: 2023947478

Cover and interior design: Jonathan Hahn
Cover photo: Courtesy of Lisa and Mitch Evans

Printed in the United States of America

For Reid

CONTENTS

AUTHOR'S NOTE

The events and dialogues recounted in this book have been recreated to the best of my ability, and are supported by numerous sources, including diary entries I made after each incident, voicemails, emails, sworn statements from myself and coworkers, transcripts of depositions, the FBI case file for my EEO complaint, and conversations with other individuals who were present. The opinions expressed are mine alone.

In some cases, names of individuals in this book have been fictionalized. Fictional names are indicated by the use of SMALL CAPS on first mention. Any similarity between the fictionalized names and the names of other real people is strictly coincidental.

1

You Had Me at Decomp

The stench of rotting flesh hit us as soon as we stepped out of the car. Once it grabbed hold, there was no escape. Hours later, I could still feel it on me, and it was several days before I stopped imagining catching whiffs of it.

Amy, our guide for the day, offered us face masks, but we all declined. If she wasn't wearing one, then we weren't either. If we had any sense, we would have accepted, but none of us wanted to look as if we couldn't handle what was coming. After all, we were from the FBI; we could tough it out.

Bug spray was another matter entirely. I wasn't about to turn that down. This wasn't just about preventing mosquito bites or Lyme disease. I knew any insects within a one-mile radius would have just finished nibbling on rotting corpses, and I wanted to keep them as far away from me as possible. A cartoon vision of a bug wiping its dirty feet on me like a welcome mat popped in my head, and I laughed to myself. It wouldn't be so funny if blow flies or maggots ended up in my hair, so I grabbed the insecticide again and kept spraying until the can hissed that it was empty.

Lavender gloves and baby blue booties were handed out next, the same kind doctors and nurses wear. For the next hour we'd be walking through mud, muck, and a host of bodily fluids.

I stared at the chain-link fence topped with coils of barbed wire. This wasn't the strongest of security measures, but then again, not too many people tried to get inside anymore. Apparently, the shock value of having hundreds of naked bodies lying out in the sun had worn off. When the Body Farm first opened in 1981 there was plenty of outrage, not to mention a few drunken teenagers scaling the fence to see inside the only facility dedicated to the study of human decomposition. Now, the residents of Knoxville, Tennessee, didn't just accept this patch of land and what it stood for; they were downright proud of it.

Amy removed the heavy metal lock from the hinge, and the gate creaked open. "After you," she said. And there it was, the wholly generic yet infamous battered metal sign propped against the fence in the dirt: ANTHROPOLOGY RESEARCH FACILITY—FOR INFORMATION CALL DR. WILLIAM BASS.

It took a moment to sink in. Not many people get to stand where we were right now, and we weren't about to take it for granted. WADE and I just looked at each other and laughed. He was a forensic artist like me, and the only other person in our group who appreciated skulls as much as I did.

Our photographer, GEOFF, had wandered off in search of photos, while KIRK, the 3D-modeling expert, assessed the surroundings. He built crime scene models for court, and his brain always worked over-time looking for a bigger, better, or faster way to build something.

Amy made her way toward a cargo van parked beside a shed. She eyed Wade and Kirk. "You guys feel like doing some heavy lifting?" They looked at each other and shrugged in agreement. When else would they get a chance to move a dead body?

"We only used to get a couple each year," Amy explained, "but now we get over a hundred. That's why this one is going straight into the freezer, at least for now."

"Freezer? Where?" I asked. All I saw were trees. Amy nodded toward a toolshed that I had mistakenly assumed contained tools. "Over there."

She held the door open while Wade and Kirk slid the body out of the van and adjusted their grip. It was wrapped in a heavy layer of white sheets and was still frozen solid, having made the three-hour trip packed in dry ice. Taking up most of the space inside the shed was a plain white freezer, the big top-loading kind that your grandmother used to have in the basement, the kind you were sure held dead bodies and monsters instead of hamburger and leftover lasagna. Here is where you realize your childhood nightmares weren't so off base after all; not only were there bodies in this freezer, but they had actually volunteered for the job.

The cadaver that Wade and Kirk were maneuvering into place was part of the Anthropology Research Facility's donated collection. When it first opened, the collection contained anonymous, unclaimed corpses acquired through the state medical examiner's office. As time went on, body donation became a viable alternative for families who were either unable to pay for a burial or chose it as a way to support research in forensic science. The facility will pick up a body within a hundred-mile radius and transport it for free.

Now there was actually a waiting list, with over four thousand willing participants preregistered for a spot on the grounds. Once the bodies are "done," their skeletons are thoroughly cleaned, packed in long cardboard boxes, and stacked on sturdy metal shelving at the university. "Any other bodies you want us to move, lady?" Kirk joked.

Amy smiled. "I think one is enough for today. So where do you want to start?" We all looked around at once. I pointed to a pair of feet with cherry-red toenail polish peeping out from under a black plastic tarp, the loose corner flapping in the breeze. "That one?" I asked.

"Sure," Amy replied. "We only put her out yesterday, but let's see what's going on under there." She knelt down and peeled back the heavy plastic. "Oh wow! See here? Something's been chewing on her legs. That didn't take long!"

We leaned in for a closer look. "So what would have done that? Rats?" I ventured.

"Sure, could be rats. Or maybe squirrels."

"Really? I thought squirrels didn't eat meat. Or at least, they didn't eat people."

"That's what I thought, too. But we've got video." Amy stood up and pointed to several cameras mounted to wooden posts. "Don't trust raccoons, either. They aren't as cute as you think they are." Amy brushed off her slacks and motioned for us to follow. "I've got another that's been out here for a few weeks. But he's deeper in the woods, in the shade."

Well, this isn't so bad, I thought. I can't exactly say that I was getting used to the smell of things, but the visuals were so surreal, and so fascinating, that I didn't have time to think of being nauseous.

My bravado wavered at our next stop. I couldn't tell whether the body was young or old, male or female, but one thing was for certain: it was *huge*.

"This one's pretty bloated, so be careful. He could go any minute." Amy said. *Please don't explode, please don't explode,* I sang to myself, as I nodded and crouched down. I'd heard that bodies in the late stages of decomposition could "pop," and in my mind Amy had just confirmed it. As it turns out, bodies don't actually explode in one spectacular burst; the skin ruptures and tears apart slowly, leaving ample time for a running head start in the opposite direction.

I inched closer to take pictures, trying my best not to breathe in too deeply. As bad as the smell was from the parking lot, it was a thousand times worse close up. It was then I saw the mass of maggots crawling around the face. Suddenly, the jokes we'd made about having tapioca for lunch didn't seem quite so funny.

By now, I was regretting not wearing a mask, but it wasn't because of the smell. This was the middle of July in Tennessee, and thousands of gnats swarmed in heavy clouds as we walked among the trees.

The thought of inhaling those tiny, venomous insects would be enough to send me over the edge. I pretended to turn my head to sneeze, tucking my nose inside the elbow of my shirt to breathe. I looked up at the bright blue sky and focused on seeing shapes in the clouds. Anything I could think of to take my mind away from the sights, smells, and sounds of human decay.

Why did maggots have to sound just like someone chewing a sandwich with their mouth open? Would this smell ever come out of my clothes? And why did it have to be so darn hot? I was desperate for a cool breeze. Whose bright idea was this, anyway? Oh, yeah; it was mine.

It's not as though I woke up one day and thought, *I want to gross myself out in the most expedient way possible.* But the project we were working on was the first of its kind, and a veritable gold mine of information for forensic artists. What we were doing could help identify thousands of bodies buried in unmarked graves and help bring closure to families searching for missing loved ones.

If you've ever seen *CSI*, then you probably imagine that forensic facial approximation is pretty straightforward. An artist glues thin rubber erasers to a skull and fills out the spaces in between with clay to create a face. The sculpture turns out to be a perfect likeness, and the victim is readily identified.

If only it were that easy. While the skull does hold clues as to what a person looks like, there are still many unknowns. And that's the part that drove me crazy. Whenever I see an interesting-looking person, I try not to stare while I think, *What is going* on *under there? Why does she have a dimple on one cheek but not the other? What causes her eyelids to fold that way? Why is her right eye higher than the left, and was she born with that nose or did plastic surgery have something to do with it?*

In a perfect world, I would be able to find answers in a photo-graphic collection of both skulls and their corresponding faces, but there was no practical way of putting one together. Forensic artists check the accuracy of our work based on the identifications we get, but we aren't able to share that information with each other. The moment a skull goes from being a number to a name, it has an iden-tity and rights, as do the decedent's family members. Artists needed real-world examples for comparison and education, but we couldn't get them without permission of the victims' relatives. And that's just something you can't ask a grieving family.

It was after reading forensic anthropologist William Bass's book *Death's Acre* that the answer came to me. I was thinking of donating my body to science, and what could be a better choice than the Body Farm? As I filled out the research facility's online donation form, I noticed a check box for submitting a driver's license photo. I blinked my eyes to make sure I wasn't seeing things. *Photos!* The Body Farm had photos of known donors! Plus they had donated *themselves*, so permission had already been granted to use them for research.

I was so excited I could barely see straight, and my mind went into overdrive: *I'm going to get a team together and go there. We'll scan every single skull and get every photo they have. We're finally going to figure some things out, and when we do, every forensic artist will know about it too!*

I envisioned advanced facial approximation classes at the FBI's training academy, with reference catalogs that could be shared among artists. Maybe even a secure, online database with 3D models of the skulls. The possibilities seemed endless, and as the Body Farm collec-tion grew, so did my enthusiasm.

I've seen some ghastly things over the years, like the carnage of a plane crash and definitive proof that having "your brains blown out" is not a euphemism. This sort of thing hadn't been covered in the job interview, and it's probably for the best, because I might have backed out had I known. But now, I could look at severed heads while eating a cranberry muffin and not think twice about it.

"How did you ever get a job like this?" It's always the first question people ask me, and I don't mean to be vague when I say it just sort of happened.

For me, it took an enlistment in the navy, and years of working in jobs I hated while earning my degree in art. Then somehow, luck, timing, and preparation converged, and I ended up landing the best, and dare I say coolest job on the planet. The job didn't come to me easily by any means, and for a long, hideous period in my career I had to fight tooth and nail to keep it.

In the bureau, there are two types of people: FBI agents, and everybody else. I was the second type, one of the thirty-five thousand support staff personnel who do exactly what the name says. If it's an agent's job to go out and catch bad guys, then it's my job to help the agent with any graphic assistance they might need.

Most people think FBI headquarters is teeming with humorless men and women in black suits. Believe it or not, agents are regular people like you and me, with friends, families, and senses of humor, and, based on the ones I worked with, are very professional and highly dedicated to their work. Most of the FBI agents actually work in one of the fifty-six field offices across the United States, or in one of the sixty-three legal attaché offices (or "legats," as they're known) around the world.

There are about 14,000 women employed by the FBI, but most of them are in support roles; only 2,700 or so are in special agent positions. Roughly half the bureau's 21,000 male employees (11,000) are agents, meaning male agents outnumber female agents four to one.

At the FBI Laboratory Division, where I worked, there are about six hundred people, and most of them are support staff. Besides the forensic artists, there are scientists, DNA analysts, geologists, anthropologists, firearms experts, photographers, cryptologists, and too many more to name.

The FBI Laboratory isn't run like the military, although as you'd expect, there are stacks of rules to abide by, procedures to follow, and even procedures for how those procedures are established. But the idea is, nobody needs to bark orders or question every decision a person makes in their work. We are professionals, we know our job, and we are expected to become subject matter experts in our chosen field.

Everything we do is on behalf of victims of crime. This sentiment was literally carved in stone when the Laboratory Division relocated to Quantico, Virginia, in 2003 from the FBI headquarters in Washington, DC. On a bed of flowers under the American and FBI flags, there is a piece of granite engraved with the agency seal and an inscription: BEHIND EVERY CASE IS A VICTIM—MAN, WOMAN, OR CHILD—AND THE PEOPLE WHO CARE FOR THEM. WE DEDICATE OUR EFFORTS AND THE NEW FBI LABORATORY BUILDING TO THOSE VICTIMS.

The contradiction inherent with being a forensic artist is that even though we create drawings and sculptures, what we produce is not art. There's no self-expression involved; our job is to produce visual information to be used within law enforcement investigations and prosecutions.

Composites are the most common and therefore best-known type of forensic art, and got their name because they are created from the parts of multiple images, and combined into one singular, cohesive face. The minute some smart aleck compared the process to being "just like Mr. Potato Head," the expression stuck, and forensic artists grimaced. I will grudgingly admit that it's a fair, but wildly oversimplified description.

The second-most common type of forensic art is age progressions. These are pretty much what they sound like: "This fugitive escaped from prison fifteen years ago, so take his arrest photo of when he was thirty-five years old and make him look like he's fifty."

But barring any new specific information about the fugitive's appearance, creating an age-progressed image boils down to educated guesswork. It's a bit like the cliché in time travel movies: what we produce is a vision of one possible future.

Composites and age progressions deal with identification of the living. Postmortem images and facial approximations deal with the identification of the dead.

A postmortem image is a photo of an unidentified deceased person that is "sanitized" with digital editing tools to make the image more appropriate to show the public. Sometimes it can be as simple as opening the eyes and closing the mouth of a photo taken in the morgue. Others are extremely challenging and can take days to retouch because of bruises, blunt force trauma, decomposition, or worse.

Facial approximation is the technique used to recreate a face based on the structure of a skull. Typically, these are only done as a last-ditch effort to identify a person, after all other means have been exhausted. For every skull an artist works on, there will be hundreds of others that will never make it to our desks.

Depending on the source (believe it or not, this gets a bit political), there are between eight thousand and forty thousand unidentified remains in the United States. In the world of TV crime dramas, a facial approximation would be done as standard procedure every time an unidentified skull is found. In reality, that's not the case, for a number of reasons: time, money, and again, politics.

The most important factor in the success of our work is you, the viewing public, and nothing illustrates this point more than the case of John List. On November 9, 1971, List shot and killed his wife, mother, and three children before disappearing. For almost two decades the case was at a standstill. Then, in 1989, *America's Most Wanted* featured an age-progressed sculpture created by the late Frank Bender. A woman in Virginia thought the sculpture bore an uncanny resemblance to her neighbor "Robert Clark," and called in a tip to the hotline. Within days, List was in handcuffs.

Every forensic artist knows this case well, and many of us have formed a love-hate relationship with it. We love that a killer was arrested, and we're thrilled that forensic art played so strong a part. What better showcase for the work that we do than to have it become so iconic that people who weren't even born at the time know about it and discuss it in true-crime forums and Facebook groups?

But I get a bit uncomfortable when people rave about it to me, because it perpetuates inaccuracies about the field. I'm not able to clear those up in a chance meeting if someone asks what I do for a living; I don't want my clarifications to come across as sour grapes.

The resounding success of Bender's work is not an aberration in the field of forensic art; it is just one of many examples of successful resolutions of our cases. Forensic artists get hits like this all the time, but typically they are not high-profile cases like List, and the artist rarely ends up on a national TV show.

For the most part, our successes go completely unnoticed by the media, and that's fine. Forensic artists don't do this work for the attention. Much of the time, it's just a Tuesday morning at the NYPD where a detective tells his buddy, "Hey, remember that composite we released yesterday for the subway stabbing? It looked so much like the guy, he turned himself in before we had time to arrest him."

Like horseshoes and hand grenades, getting close counts in forensic art. Whether it's a composite sketch, age progression, postmortem, or facial approximation, if we can get *close* to what a person looks like, there is a good chance that case can be solved. The work can be a maddening, frustrating mix of luck and timing, but there's no other job in the world I would rather do.

———————

I had no idea what a big deal it was to become a full-time forensic artist. Of course, I knew the FBI itself was a big deal, but I never knew what a small, almost miniscule field forensic art is. While there are thousands of medical examiners, crime scene investigators, and police officers in the United States, there are only about fifty full-time forensic artists. That's an educated guess. Nobody knows for sure how many of us are around because there's no official organization or certification board that governs our field. It's essentially up to each agency to hire the right person with the right skills for the job.

Full-time forensic artists are also on staff at the Central Intelligence Agency and US Secret Service, and in some large-city police departments like New York, Los Angeles, and Detroit. The common denominator is that they work at law enforcement agencies. Because forensic artists are part of active, ongoing criminal investigations, we're trained to work within the legal system, follow certain protocols, maintain the chain-of-custody for evidence (including skulls and sketches), and to be able to testify in court about our work. The only exception is the National Center for Missing and Exploited Children, a non-profit agency in Alexandria, Virginia, where forensic artists create facial approximations and age progressions of children.

Beyond those fifty or so full-time forensic artists, though, there are a few hundred others in law enforcement who do this work—largely composite drawings—as just one element of their job. Most are in "sworn" positions (police officer, detective, etc.), but there are plenty with civilian jobs—evidence technicians, crime analysts, and dispatchers—who were able to snag artist duties in their agency, simply because they were in the room when a detective asked, "Anyone know where to get a sketch artist?"

I've never met a forensic artist who shrugged at the work they did. They are fiercely committed to helping victims, often paying for their own training classes and working hours of overtime without complaint.

"I can't imagine retiring, not as long as I can hold a pencil," they'll say. And I used to say that too.

2

Walter Brown's Daughter

Working in any field related to death or crime was never something I'd considered as a career path. When anybody asked me what I wanted to be when I grew up, I couldn't answer, because I didn't know.

I remember watching police shows like *Dragnet* and *Hawaii Five-0* with my dad and would see episodes where an artist created a composite sketch that helped catch the bad guy. One time, a sculptor recreated a dead person's face from a skull, and they used it to find out who the killer was. How cool was that?

But it never occurred to me that forensic art might be a job that I could seriously pursue, even though art was my favorite subject in school. For one thing, I had no idea how to go about getting a job like that, and nobody else did either, not even the guidance counselor. I just put it out of my mind as one of those dream vocations, like the people who get paid to eat ice cream or shop for a living.

As much as I loved art, I hated science to an equal degree, and I did everything in my power to get out of any assignment that required it. Anything to do with blood or gore was off the table. The thought of dissecting a frog horrified me, so my lab partner agreed to do it if I handled writing the report. In the end, I decided to sculpt a frog instead, lying on its back pinned down to a silver tray (aluminum foil over a shoebox lid). Then I "dissected" it, making intestines by rolling out clay, coiling them up, and painting them pink, and carefully placing them in the cavity left behind from the Y-shaped incision. We both got an A for ingenuity, and I kept formaldehyde and frog guts off my hands in the process.

By the time I graduated high school, I still had no idea what I was going to do for a job. Art should have been at the top of the list, but I couldn't afford college. I went as far as getting loan applications, but the sheer expense made me gasp. Even if I got a degree, what would I do with it? I wasn't a competitive person, so I couldn't see myself working in an ad agency, and selling paintings on the street wouldn't make a dent in paying off college loans.

Joining the military seemed the best—if not only—path for me at the time. I had spent the majority of my childhood in Delaware, where my dad worked as a jet engine mechanic at Dover Air Force Base. There weren't many other career options in Dover in the late 1970s. If you didn't head off to college, you either got a job at the Playtex factory or worked at the Blue Hen Mall on Route 13.

My oldest brother, Jeff, joined the air force right after high school, and retired as a master sergeant after traveling the world. He had married the love of his life while stationed in Germany and was happy to settle in Dover, where he had a whole second career as a reporter for the local newspaper.

Ken went to the army recruiter at our local mall, thinking he might enlist too. He had an eye condition that made him ineligible, which turned out to be a blessing. He was a gentle soul, too trusting of people who didn't deserve it, and just wasn't cut out for a life in the military.

Steve enlisted in the marines the day after receiving his high school diploma, sending our mom into fits while our dad winked and gave him the thumbs-up. Neither of them had any idea what he was up to when he had asked to borrow the car, but that was pure Steve. He had nerves of steel and a wicked sense of humor, and once he made his mind up, there was little chance of anyone changing it.

My big sister, Lauren, served in the air force, joining as a jet engine mechanic just like our dad. That took some serious moxie. This was 1977, and nice young ladies, especially beautiful ones like my sister, weren't typically crawling around inside the guts of a C-141 and getting axle grease under their nails. We shared a room growing up and could never keep a squabble going on for very long, because at the end of the day we had to deal with each other in a 120-square-foot bedroom. Sooner or later, one of us would forget that we were mad at the other and we were back to being best friends.

My mom, too, had served in the Women's Army Corps until she became pregnant with Jeff. Maternity leave was unheard of then, so she happily accepted an honorable discharge and left the service to become a full-time wife and mother. My mom was also an extremely talented artist; she had worked in the art department at *Vogue* in the '40s and would do freelance work while my dad was in the service. Cartoons were her specialty. Not only did she have a bestselling book on military life published by the *Stars and Stripes*, she had a weekly cartoon strip in a local paper.

I chose the navy for no other reason than that they had the cutest uniforms. The recruiter tried to talk me into joining the nuclear weapons program—I'm sure it had more to do with meeting his quota than any potential ability on my part—but since I had only passed algebra by the skin of my teeth, that was out of the question.

I had scored well enough on the aptitude test to qualify for the intelligence field, and that was the first thing that would set me on the path to becoming a forensic artist: I was granted a security clearance. Even though I had never taken any language before, I decided to join as a Russian linguist.

After boot camp it was on to the Defense Language Institute in Monterey, California, where I was immersed in the Russian language for eight hours a day, five days a week, for forty-seven weeks, and maintained an A average without too much trouble. I can only credit my right-brain artist's mind that I didn't have a tougher time of it. I could close my eyes and picture the words and definitions on the vocabulary list when I was stumped during a test.

Language school was one thing, but applying the language in the real world of the military was another. Back then, women weren't allowed to fly or serve on ships—those were considered combat—and that's where the real work of a linguist was. My first two years of active duty I ended up doing data-processing work. I had no training for it, and even less interest, so none of it made any sense, and I hated every second of it.

Thankfully, my transfer to a military base in Turkey changed all that, and I was able to do some semblance of the work I had spent over a year and a half training for. I'm indebted to the navy for helping me transition from a wildly insecure girl to a fairly levelheaded adult, but a career in the military, at least as a Russian linguist, wasn't for me.

In 1987, I was back in the states when my six-year enlistment ended, and I needed a job, fast. The only thing I really had going for me was my very high level of security clearance, which is a highly prized commodity in the Washington, DC, area. Lots of people have a secret clearance, but to be designated TS/SCI w/Poly (top-secret clearance and a clean polygraph test)? Pure gold.

Most of my family was still in Delaware, so I packed up a Nissan Sentra with two loudly meowing, highly tranquilized cats in the backseat and headed east. I had a job within a week, working as a data processor in a contract position at the Johns Hopkins University Applied Physics Laboratory in Maryland. I was grateful to have found work so quickly, but it was dry, repetitive work, and it didn't take long for me to become bored.

So now what? I was twenty-seven years old, a military veteran, and I still didn't know what I wanted to be when I grew up. I was scouring the job boards hoping to find something that would inspire me. That's when I saw a posting for a graphic artist, creating conceptual artwork for the scientists in the Applied Physics Laboratory's Submarine Technology Department. It never occurred to me that the government would have the need for an artist, and as I read the posting I got more and more interested. There was only one hitch: it required an art degree.

I had a few credits from classes I had taken while I was in the navy and knew that going to college while working full-time was going to take forever. But now I had a goal, and my mind was made up. I was going to finish college, get the hell out of data processing, and become a graphic artist at Johns Hopkins.

But there was a problem. Just as I couldn't afford college as a teenager, I couldn't afford it now either. Even though I worked at Hopkins, I was a contractor, not professional staff, so I didn't qualify for its college tuition benefits. My only choice was to get a second job, working part-time at a video store for the extra money. I took one night class each semester, and the other nights I worked at Blockbuster.

Not surprisingly, I also couldn't afford a computer to do my homework, so I started going to the Hopkins media lab during lunch where they had a fleet of Macintosh computers and all the graphic software that went along with them. That's where I met the first person who would change the trajectory of my career, the manager of the media lab, Dan. After a few weeks of seeing me there, he said "There's someone I need you to meet."

That woman was Barbara Williamson, the supervisor of the art department, who took me under her wing as I learned Freehand, Photoshop, and everything else it would take to become an artist at Hopkins. When a data processing job opened in her group—a staff position with tuition benefits—she helped me land the job. Now I could quit the video store and take two classes per semester instead of one.

A few weeks before my graduation, she called me into her office where there was a surprise party waiting for me. Barb handed me a letter with the news that I had been officially promoted as an artist-illustrator. Working under Barb in the art department was the most fun I ever had in my life at work, and everyone there grew to feel like family to me.

Dan was the genius who kept our computers, software, and thousands of graphic presentations organized and up to date. This was back in the days of floppy disks and Bernoulli drives, the computer equivalent to 8-track tapes, so it was no small feat. A scientist could come to our door looking for a presentation we had done three years before, and with Dan's sophisticated archive system we could put our hand on it in seconds. He was funny, kind, and quirky, and when we got the Internet and e-mail, he sat down with a pen and paper and patiently explained to me how it all worked.

Cathy did the desktop publishing, but she could have worked right beside us as one of the artists. She was a terrific oil painter and had an innate sense of composition and design. Don shared my love of kitsch, snarky humor, and midcentury modern design and illustration. We could have an hour-long discussion on what our favorite fonts were and why, and we both knew the lyrics to Disney and Pixar movies by heart. Kevin reminded me of my brother Steve; he had the same devilish sense of humor, and was a stickler for quality and perfection in his work. Robin was the one with the dry wit. Panicked clients would often come in wailing, "Can you have this done in an hour? I really need it now!" When they finally strolled in a week later, Robin would calmly hand the stack of papers back to them while saying, "Oh, let me brush the dust off your rush job first." Brilliant.

Barb was the woman who made the whole operation sing. She was a phenomenal artist in her own right, and never forgot that when you supervise a group of artists you need to give them the freedom and mental space to create. She made sure everyone in the department knew what a crackerjack team she had, and felt it was her duty to help us grow in our career. She was fiercely protective, and nobody, not even a rocket scientist, could get away with talking down to or taking advantage of us. "Listen here, Bucko, you can't come in here every Friday at 5:00 PM and expect my artists to work late just because you can't manage your time better!" And you better believe, they listened.

It was an atmosphere of professionalism, teamwork, creativity, and joy, and became an oasis for some of the physicists and scientists when they needed to step away from their desk. Does it sound like nirvana? It was. And I never wanted anything to change.

───────────

One fateful day, I spotted an ad in the *Washington Post* with the heading FBI ARTIST-ILLUSTRATOR WANTED. I wasn't thinking of leaving Hopkins, but I was fascinated by what I *could* be doing at the bureau. Trial exhibits for court, composite sketches, documenting crime scenes, travel. This was an opportunity to draw all day and help catch bad guys? It was too good to be true.

Still, in the DC area it's common knowledge that federal postings aren't always real. Usually, the best jobs are filled internally, but for legal reasons the agency has to post them for the public. You know, to make the process fair. But it was like this posting had been written with my résumé in hand: I already had the top-secret clearance with a clear polygraph, I had the drawing ability, bachelor's degree, and I knew Freehand, Photoshop, and PowerPoint (the graphic art trifecta at the time). I had tons of design experience, was used to working under extremely tight deadlines, and even worked with a few 3D-modeling programs.

But I really struggled to decide whether I should apply. I loved everyone at Hopkins, but I also knew that anybody could leave at any time. Being a military kid taught me that. Every three years, my best friend would move because her dad had been sent to another part of the country or world. Finally, I decided I had nothing to lose by trying. I probably wouldn't get it, but at least I'd see the inside of the FBI and have a good story to tell my friends.

I put my résumé and cover letter in a FedEx envelope and sent it off. As months rolled by without a peep from Washington, I assumed that someone else had gotten the job. I had never considered no news might be good news. But then one day when I was working on a rush job, the phone rang. It was a very nice man who said his name was RON, and he was from the FBI. The connection didn't quite register in my mind, and I assumed it was time for my five-year security clearance update.

I half-listened while trying to keep working on my deadline, and then I heard him say, "You made the cut." My heart did a little flip as I remembered the application I had sent off nine months earlier. He went on to tell me that they had received a few hundred applications and they had narrowed it down to several candidates. When would I be available for an interview?

Gulp. It was going to be a phone interview, so we set it up for the next day. This was before anyone except Hollywood producers had cell phones, and I didn't want to call during work hours. I put in a request for annual leave and went home early. Right on the dot, the phone rang, and there were four other people on speaker phone who would be interviewing me as well.

Everyone was super nice, and I was asked varying questions about my software knowledge and methods for tackling design problems. The only difficulty was that I was home and didn't have a computer in front of me. One of the first questions was "How would you fix a blurry photo?"

Just like I did when I was learning Russian, I closed my eyes to see the Photoshop menu in my head and started going through the process. "OK, first I'd go to Filter, Sharpen, Unsharp Mask, click the preview mode button, then I'd adjust the radiance, threshold and . . ." If your eyes just glazed over, I don't blame you, but to a table of artists it sounded like I knew what I was talking about.

Ron asked if I had a website so they could see my portfolio. I didn't, so he asked if I could put something together on a Zip drive (this was 1998) and send it to him by the end of the next week. "Sure," I said. There were only two problems: One, I hadn't put a portfolio together. Since so much time had gone by, I thought my application was in the reject pile. And two, I didn't have a home computer. But one Visa card and twenty-four hours later, those problems were solved. I bought a Bondi Blue iMac and stayed up late every night putting together my portfolio.

I thought I was in for another months-long waiting period, but within the week I got the call. "The job is yours, if you want it." Really?! I thought the phone interview was just the first step in the process. Ironically, I had gotten the job without even seeing what the inside of the FBI looked like.

Soon, FBI agents were interviewing my neighbors, coworkers, and friends from high school, and I was taking polygraphs and drug tests. Things were moving at lightning speed and then screeched to a halt on September 30, 1999, the end of the fiscal year. The rush had been to try to get me in before a rumored hiring freeze. As it turned out, the rumor was true, and nobody had any idea when it would be over.

I spent the next two years anxiously waiting and wondering. Every three or four months I would call Ron or he would call me, just to check in and remind each other that I was, in fact, going to be a new bureau employee. Finally, the freeze lifted, and the FBI hiring machine started back up. It was a Baltimore field agent who shook my hand on Friday, September 7, 2001, and said, "Welcome to the bureau." There was still some paperwork left to handle, but I was as good as in.

Until the catastrophic events of that Tuesday. I naturally assumed the FBI had bigger things to handle after 9/11, so I called Ron and told him I was still prepared to wait. He assured me that hiring efforts were being stepped up, and most likely I would be in before Christmas.

He was right. My start date at the FBI was November 4, 2001. It had been three years since I first sent in my résumé. Three years of wondering if I had just dreamed that I had gotten the job of a lifetime, and three years of people asking, "Are you *sure* the FBI said they were going to hire you?" As the years of waiting passed, I had begun wondering that myself. But I stuck it out, and it finally paid off.

Whenever I thought of giving up during those three years, I would think of my dad. And I think of how proud he would be to know that his daughter, his baby girl, had ended up working at the most respected, powerful law enforcement agency in the world.

Walter Edgar Brown Jr. grew up in Tower City, Pennsylvania, the only son of a coal miner among three sisters, during the Depression. Even though he passed away from a heart attack in 1993, he was then and continues to be the single most important influence in my life.

Not a day goes by that I don't think of him, wonder what he would do in a difficult situation, or find words coming out of my mouth that he would say. What he taught me, by just being himself, made me who I am today.

How did he do this? How did he influence the direction my life took, teach me about right and wrong, and what it meant to be a decent human being? In a ton of different ways, and all really very simple.

First, acceptance. He loved all of us kids exactly as we were, and thoroughly enjoyed being around us. He never had to "escape" into another room to get away from all the craziness in the house; he was right there in the middle of it all, and that was exactly where he wanted to be.

When we screwed up, when we realized, *Maybe that didn't work out so well after all,* he was always there for us. But not to rescue us. He gave us the opportunity to do things for ourselves, mess up, learn something from it, and usually laugh about it too. He always encouraged us to do better, but there was never any pressure. "Just do the best you can," he'd say, "That's all that you can ask of yourself."

When I asked him what I should be when I grew up, he told me, "You can be whatever you want to be, but no matter what you do, always do your best. I don't care if you dig ditches for a living, just do it well." If I had a job I loved, I would be very lucky, but even if I didn't, I should still give it my all. After all, nobody is irreplaceable. There would be plenty of people standing in line to take my place if I left, and "that's why they pay you and call it a job."

He had a great sense of humor. He appreciated a quick wit, and never laughed harder than when one of us kids made a wisecrack, especially at his expense. It was like we were honing our comedic skills, just so we could get him to laugh.

He never yelled, *ever.* Seven people living in a small house could frazzle anybody's nerves, but not my dad. Lauren and I shared a bedroom, and our mom was always after us to clean it up. This is what my dad did. He opened the door to our bedroom, looked around at the clothes hanging over the purple bunk bed, and teen magazines, nail polish, candy wrappers, and bags of malted milk balls all over the pink shag carpet, then said very calmly with a genuine look of concern, "Was anybody hurt?"

"What?" we said, clearly not getting it.

"You know, was anybody hurt when the bomb went off?"

We'd giggle and say, *"Da-a-a-addy!"* and the room got cleaned. That was my dad. Why yell when you can make a joke?

He had a very strong work ethic. He was in the air force for twenty-six years, and I only remember him being out sick once. He was working on a plane when he slipped and fell off the wing, slicing his head open in the process. It's a wonder that was all that happened, and of course he joked and said it was all thanks to his hard head that he didn't get worse.

He was nice to everyone, "unless someone gave him a reason not to be." It didn't matter if you were the CEO or someone emptying the trash, you were treated the same. And he couldn't go anywhere without bumping into people he knew, either someone he had just seen the week before, but still had time to tell a joke, or an old buddy that he had been with in Vietnam.

He was the most easygoing man in the world, but never a pushover. He knew how to pick his battles. He told me a number of times growing up, "There is a certain amount of horseshit you have to put up with in this world. Just don't let anybody rub your face in it."

So when confronted with a dilemma, I examine it from all sides and then decide whether it's the hill I want to die on. Often, it's not. But when I know that a line has been crossed, when I know something is just plain wrong, I will fight back with everything I have in me, and I will *not—back—down*. That's a trait that I got from my dad, and for better or worse, it's one that would have a major influence on my life in the FBI.

3

Whole New World

Objectively, the J. Edgar Hoover Building, as FBI headquarters is officially named, is one of the ugliest buildings in Washington, DC. But on my first day of work it was the most beautiful sight in the world. I'd learned in art history class that it belongs to the "brutalist" style of architecture, and boy, they weren't kidding. Completed in 1975, the building is a stark, bland, concrete behemoth that sits like a lump on Pennsylvania Avenue, less than a mile from the White House.

The first few days on the job are the same as for any new government hire: orientation. There were countless forms for me to fill out, papers to sign, and poorly acted videos on sexual harassment to watch. When I thought I couldn't stand the suspense any longer, I met my new unit chief, Ron. For the past three years, it had all been phone calls and emails.

He greeted me at the guard station, then took me through a maze of stark white hallways with battered linoleum flooring, and to my new home, the Graphic Unit. Hey, where's all the slick furniture? The chrome spiral staircases and backlit frosted-glass cabinets? What about the wind machines?

Of course, I didn't really expect anything *that* impressive. The images you see of FBI workspaces come purely out of a TV writer's imagination. To put it nicely, the unit was dingy, with carpet worn down to the burlap, rust-colored stains on the ceiling, and the faint scent of mold in the air. All my adult life I had worked in offices without windows, and the basement of the FBI was no exception.

After we walked past a rack of blue jackets with "FBI" emblazoned on the backs in bright yellow, we came to a nondescript gray locker where Ron told me they stored the skulls. *Excuse me?* I knew the FBI did some cool things, but skulls in a locker? This was awesome!

"Um, so, how many skulls are in there?" I asked.

"It depends," Ron shrugged. "Sometimes we get two or three a year for facial approximation. They're unidentified remains cases, usually homicides, and we work with anthropologists at the Smithsonian to create them. You'll go to class to learn how to do that, if you want."

Of course I wanted! Who wouldn't want to get their hands on a skull? This was supremely surreal to me. I had never seen a real human skull outside a museum, and now I'd be working with them, hands-on, and the thought didn't bother me a bit. I was actually excited.

Then Ron stopped in front of a wall of artwork, displaying row after row of tightly rendered composite drawings—cold, staring faces of people suspected of some of the worst crimes imaginable. I had seen images like these on TV and in the news, most notoriously up to that point, Timothy McVeigh, the Oklahoma City bomber. *One of the artists in this unit did this sketch!* my brain shouted.

Ron continued the tour, pointing out complex diagrams of money-laundering schemes and outlines of bodies on floor plans of apartments. He explained that the 3D illustrations of torsos riddled with stab wounds were created to prevent the jury from having to see actual images that were too messy to decipher, or so gruesome that the defense attorney might have them ruled inadmissible. Not only do forensic artists need to have a number of software skills, they need to have a strong stomach as well.

Ron introduced me to GARY MORGAN, who would be my immediate supervisor. Gary was extremely intimidating to me at first, but it turns out he's the friendliest guy in the world with an arsenal of war stories, and exactly the person you want to sit next to in an airport bar after your flight has been delayed for the umpteenth time. By the time your plane boards, you'll forget why you were ever angry.

He also has a sarcastic sense of humor, which I fully appreciated. It's a survival tool you need in a big family, and it's especially valuable in law enforcement or the military. Both fields are overwhelmingly male, with good-natured ribbing and insults being thrown around. Besides, I had seen every Marx Brothers movie with my dad multiple times and knew some great Groucho zingers by heart.

I don't think everyone in the unit appreciated his type of humor, but I found there wasn't any malice behind his remarks. I had only been there a month when he came up to my desk while I was flipping through a large city map, with my feet resting on a small filing cabinet. "Working hard, I see." Without thinking, I said "Yup, and I'm going to paint my toenails after this." *Oh shit! I was just a wise ass with my boss, and I was still under probation!* I was starting to explain that I was kidding, and I wasn't goofing off at all, I just needed to look up a street name for a map I was working on, but he was already walking away chuckling.

There's a learning curve in starting in any new job, but coming into the Graphic Unit in 2001 was like being transported back to the dark ages of computer technology. If you needed to Google anything, you had to elbow your way past the other artists in the unit waiting to get a spot at one of the two Internet stations. I kid you not. There was a grand total of two Internet stations for all eighteen artists to share.

Scanners were another precious commodity. When I worked at Hopkins, each of us had a scanner at our workstation, and it wasn't considered a luxury item. Imagine my surprise when I get to the FBI expecting the most up-to-date and cutting-edge equipment known to man, only to find out that I have to wait in line at the one scanner we all shared.

None of the software was up to date either, owing to lack of funding (thanks, Congress) and the ridiculous amount of security hoops our software administrator had to jump through. On the bright side, all the computers were Macs (that's an artist thing), but even then, they had seen better days.

All combined, this made it especially hard on the artists who had been churning out high-level presentations at breakneck speed for FBI director Robert Mueller for weeks on end. At the time, PENTTBOM (the codename for the September 11 attacks) was the No. 1 priority at the FBI, and the Graphic Unit was no exception. The artists had been working twelve-hour shifts to keep the presentations going around the clock. Traffic in DC is notoriously awful, so some opted to sleep at work until their next shift. There was no point spending four hours driving to only get four hours sleep at home.

Several artists had been on-site doing survey work while the Pentagon was literally still burning. Other artists were on the scene as well, documenting for the trial charts to come, including gut-wrenching interactive presentations of the last moments of the passengers on those doomed flights. There were voicemails from office workers trapped in the World Trade Center towers, which had to be played over and over and over to get the transcription down correctly.

The unit was back to a regular eight-hour schedule by the time I started, but there was still an avalanche of work to be done on PENTTBOM, including the prosecution of Zacarias Moussaoui, a suspected would-be hijacker. Over three thousand images of the victims from the attacks needed to be digitized and retouched. Some of the images were on CDs, sent in from agents in the field, but there were also stacks and stacks of hard copies that needed to be scanned.

There must have been digital versions of the photos somewhere, but it wasn't as easy as you'd think to track them down.

If we couldn't find a person's photo online, then we had to scan the paper copy. Usually, it was a second- or third-generation image, because the originals had been returned to the families. It was frustrating to not have the best image possible, since nobody wanted it to seem like we hadn't done all we could to make the presentations professional and dignified.

We spent hours and hours scanning and cleaning up images and, not surprisingly, it was incredibly draining work. We were scanning pictures of birthday parties, weddings, and high school graduations— all the happiest moments of a person's life. We had a list of who the victims were, but the process was complicated by the fact many of these were group photos, so we couldn't be sure who had survived and who hadn't. Often, there was a main marker circled around one person, meaning that was the victim whose name was on the photo. Sometimes, we'd get photos on which nothing was circled and would come to the realization that everyone in the photo was gone.

———————

When I wasn't working on PENTTBOM, I was doing brochures, diagrams, and timelines. I especially loved doing demonstrative evidence, the graphic presentation of the facts of the case to the jury. For example, a bloody glove is evidence. A scale diagram of a bloody glove lying next to a fence where OJ says he didn't drop it would be demonstrative evidence.

I threw everything I had into the work, studying news magazines with phenomenal graphics that illustrated the article. Before the Internet, artists use to keep a physical "morgue" of photos and magazine clippings to use as reference in the work. I did the same thing, and kept them in binders for reference and ideas. I'm an artist with hyperperfectionist wiring, so it was really satisfying work to make sense of a complicated subject, while also making it visually compelling to hold someone's attention.

But one of the unwritten rules in the FBI was to not make the presentations look "too good." The worry was that it would seem like the defendant didn't have a chance against the deep pockets and never-ending resources of the government. In the courtroom, making a splashy over-the-top presentation might do more harm than good.

Another thing we were told to avoid was the use of bright colors, especially red. Defense attorneys had been known to object to exhibits with red lettering, especially during a homicide case. "Too much like blood" was the reasoning, a subliminal reminder of the crime scene photos.

During my interview for the job, I remember being asked if the sight of blood would bother me. "We deploy to crime scenes," Ron said, "so it's fairly certain that you'll see a good deal of it."

"I can handle that," I said and then paused, not sure whether to ask this next question: "Are the bodies still there?"

"No, by the time we get there, the bodies have usually been documented and taken to the morgue. We're there to do more detailed measurements of the scene itself in order to build models and do presentations."

I had never been in a room with blood spatter and who knows what else on the walls, but I was pretty sure I could handle it. The job just sounded so absolutely fascinating I wasn't going to let that bother me. But after I had been there a few months, several of the other artists started telling horror stories about how I would have to go to airplane crashes while all the bodies—and parts of them—were still there.

WHAT? OK, this was *not* what they said in the interview, and I was horrified. I'm not a great flyer, and seeing that type of carnage up close, stepping over and between bodies, made me shudder. I didn't know if I could do *that*.

I wasn't about to quit, but frankly I was shaken up. I talked to my husband, Reid, and he said it sounded like they were just trying to scare me. "Don't worry about it until the time comes, and by then you may not think anything about it."

He turned out to be right, of course. My first time seeing death up close was a plane crash that had killed the pilot and several passengers. A senior artist had done the surveying work and 2D diagrams, and now the agent wanted an interactive presentation to go along with it. It wouldn't be going to trial, so there wasn't an issue about me having to testify. But I was a bit hesitant about what I would be seeing.

"This is nothing" the artist said, waving off my hesitation. "You'll be seeing a lot worse if you make it through probation."

I didn't want her to think I was being a coward, but c'mon, this wasn't a movie; it was real life. Five people were dead, chewed up in a plane crash, and I was about to see all of it.

Steeling myself for what was to come, I started focusing on the outside of the debris field and slowly worked my way in. The yellow markers from the scene told me where the smaller bits would be and, as I zoomed in, I thought, *She's right, this isn't so bad.*

Then things took a turn for the worse. *Oh . . . that looks like part of a finger. And is that a foot? Or part of one?*

I got my first real shock as I inched my way closer to the impact site, coming face-to-face with . . . a face. It was impossible to tell what the person looked like, because the skin had literally been blown off the skull. It looked like a torn Halloween mask that had been thrown on the ground, but what was most unsettling was that there was still a necktie around the collar.

I didn't freak out, though, or even get nauseated. A part of my brain just went, *Huh. Well, would you look at that?* For the time being the image in front of me had stopped being a person. It was just pixels on a screen.

———————————

I hadn't been there a year when Gary grabbed a brown paper sack out of a locker and told me that we were going to the Smithsonian. I'm sure that anyone who saw us walking down Pennsylvania Avenue never gave a second thought to what might have been in that bag, but I knew it must have been a skull.

Whose skull turned out to be the exciting part. We were going to meet with the Smithsonian anthropologist to do a superimposition of a skull that they'd hoped belonged to the most-wanted terrorist of all time, Osama Bin Laden. This was in early 2002, and the best "technology" for the job required it to be done in a very old-school, clunky way.

Very simply, a still image of Bin Laden was projected onto a screen while Gary held the skull and tried to orient it to fit his face. This takes a lot of trial and error, especially when you have no idea whether it's the right skull and the right face. But that was the point. If there was any possibility that this was the man himself, then the military (and President Bush too, I guess) wanted to know about it.

After a while, Gary's arms got tired, and he held the skull out to me: "Wanna give it a shot?"

You bet I did! This was my first time ever holding a real human skull, and better than that, it might be of the Al Qaeda ringleader himself. But after a few hours, it was clear to the Smithsonian anthropologist that it could not possibly be him. If the skull had lined up with the features and structure of Bin Laden's face well enough to consider that there was a *possibility* of it being Bin Laden, then further efforts would be taken to confirm that.

But it was a moot point. Still, it was an incredible experience, and I'm thankful to Gary that he included me in it. It just confirmed in my mind even more that skulls, and facial approximation, was where my interest lay.

Every year the Graphic Unit taught a crime scene class to state and local police agencies as part of the FBI Laboratory's training program. It was free of charge to each agency, from the airfare to the meals to the dorm rooms the students would stay in. Yes, this was an expensive venture for the bureau, but it made sense in the long run to ensure that law enforcement agencies were all on the same page—using the same diagramming techniques and vernacular. It also helped with getting agencies to collaborate. Once you spend a week digging up a (fake) corpse, you can make working friendships for life.

I was the only bureau employee in a sea of patrol officers, homicide detectives, and first responders in a class called Crime Scene Diagramming and Documentation. To say I was intimidated would be a monumental understatement. I had never been anywhere near a crime scene, and I worried they would think I was some kind of mole. After all, my boss's boss, Ron, was the head instructor. But I shouldn't have worried, and I soon became one of the most popular people in the class, for one simple reason: I had a car.

Every student got to the academy by way of the plain white FBI bus that picked them up at Ronald Reagan Washington National Airport. Once you were dropped off in front of the administration building, you were there for the duration.

Each night, five classmates would pile into my cobalt-blue VW bug that was designed to hold four, and off we'd go to the mall or any other place that wasn't serving government food. We never went for a beer run, because alcohol is prohibited in the academy dorms.

Even if you weren't bureau, "Fidelity, Bravery, and Integrity" was taken seriously, and if you didn't have the integrity to follow the rules, the FBI didn't want you there.

The only place you could drink at the academy was called the Boardroom, easily the most popular spot to be in the evening after classes ended and the chow hall emptied out. I ate in the chow hall once, and that was enough. It's not like the food was horrible, but I don't eat meat, and there was precious little at the cafeteria that wasn't smothered in beef broth or swimming in bacon fat.

Happily, the Boardroom had pizza. Granted, it was the frozen, cardboard, single-serve pizza you'd get at a bowling alley, but with a great big salad and a glass of chardonnay, I was all set.

Nobody is a stranger at the FBI Academy. No one sits at a table alone unless you've made it clear you prefer it that way. If you're at the academy you're in the club, and if you're standing there like a new kid nervously holding your lunch tray, someone will soon wave you over to join them.

The first thing I noticed when I sat down was that there were popcorn kernels all over the table. *Boy, these cops are messy,* I thought, and went to brush them into the trash with my napkin. Instead, the kernels flew away. These were actually ladybugs, but they weren't cute and bright and red like they're supposed to be. Ladybugs in Quantico are tan and brown and look like they're wearing marine camouflage. There were ladybugs in the showers, ladybugs crawling on the ceiling, and dead ladybugs who weren't paying attention when I got up in the middle of the night to go to the bathroom. The very next day, I bought a pair of slippers, so I didn't feel them crunch.

Beyond having a car, there was one other reason I was accepted into the class: I could draw, and that comes in very handy at a crime scene.

"Hey Lisa, why don't you draw the inside of the kitchen with all the blood on the walls?"

"Hey Lisa, how about you draw the dead lady in the grave?"

"Hey Lisa, how about you take a crack at drawing that car with all the bullet holes in it?"

This class was next to the academy in a spot called Hogan's Alley. The area looked just like a Hollywood backlot of a small town, complete with used car dealership, motel, and even a movie theater called the Biograph. History buffs will remember that as the spot where FBI agents gunned down John Dillinger as he walked out of the theater, moments after seeing *Manhattan Melodrama*. That title is still on the marquee, proving that the FBI does have some sense of humor after all.

If you've seen *Silence of the Lambs*, then you've actually seen Hogan's Alley; it's shown at about the thirty-five-minute mark when Clarisse finds out that Buffalo Bill has struck again. You can see the Dogwood Motel and All-Med Pharmacy on the left, and even some warehouses in the background. The Biograph is just out of range, on the right behind Clarisse, and like all the buildings in Hogan's Alley, housed real, working FBI offices.

These weren't facades; they are all solid brick-and-mortar buildings used to train agents year-round, to give them as close to real-life scenarios of hostage situations or gunfights with criminals (role players hired by the FBI) as possible.

I learned fairly quickly that I wasn't a natural at documenting crime scenes. I was fine on the drawing part; what I kept forgetting were simple things, like to look around before backing up and stepping on a bullet casing or bloody footprint accidentally. I was also at a loss when it came to figuring out anything to do with math or geometry. The only thing I remember about the Pythagorean theorem was when the Scarecrow recited it after getting his brains in *The Wizard of Oz*, and he got it wrong anyway.

Thank goodness the job wasn't going to be all isosceles triangles and square roots. Standing over an open grave in the woods of Hogan's Alley, scribbling like mad to keep up with my classmates, I knew the best part of my training was to come.

————————

Before 9/11 the bureau used to be focused on white-collar crime, and the Graphic Unit did lots of composites for bank robberies. As in, lots and lots. I've seen the stack of composites in the graphic file room and not only were the drawings of portrait quality, but the suspects were also all quite dapper, often depicted wearing fedoras and three-piece suits.

All the artists worked at headquarters, so it wasn't feasible, either money- or manpower-wise, to fly an artist to the scene every time someone decided to knock over a bank. What to do? Here's what the bureau came up with, and it was a process that worked phenom-enally well: thousands of mug shots that had accumulated over the years were gathered and then sorted into categories—large nose, small chin, etc.—and made into a catalog stored in three-ring binders. This became the FBI Facial Identification Catalog. The first one the FBI produced was forty years ago, literally pasted together from thousands of mug shots from across the country. There were no names attached, just alphanumeric codes for reference.

FBI agents are well trained in interviewing suspects but are just as highly trained in interviewing victims. When talking to a witness or a victim of a crime, the atmosphere in the room is much more relaxed, and the main goal is to set the victim at ease. The agent's demeanor is friendly and accommodating, and the interview is more of a conversation, but one where you want the victim to do most of the talking. After all, they're the one with all the information.

Most people, myself included, doubt that they'd ever be able to give enough of a description for a composite, but here's the secret: the catalog. Once the witness is relaxed, the agent would ask them to do a free recollection of the unidentified subject. "Just tell us anything you can remember about the man you saw in the alley."

If the witness described a person with a square face, the agent would guide the witness to the "head shape" section of the catalog, and flip past "average, round, triangular, etc." until he came to the "square head shape" page. There are sixteen photos to a page, all with different types of square heads, and the witness could pick the one that looked most familiar to them. The agent would note it on the FD-383, the official FBI form used for composite sketches. On and on the process went, back and forth with the agent taking notes until the form was filled out with everything from face shape and scars, to wrinkles and hairstyle. Once it was completed as much as it could be, the form was faxed to the artist at headquarters.

The artist had the same catalog as the agent, so a rough sketch would be put together and faxed back to the agent for the witness to review. Depending on the circumstances, the artist and witness could discuss revisions to the sketch over the phone and send several versions back and forth via fax until the witness was satisfied with the image.

Obviously, this takes longer than the two or three hours a face-to-face interview with the artist would take, but not when you factor in that the artist didn't have to get on a plane and fly out there. It wasn't feasible to have an artist on staff at each of the FBI field offices either, because there's no way to predict when and where the next robbery might be—not to mention how hard it would be to find that many artists who made it through the '60s and were able to pass the drug test.

For years, this is how composites were done in the bureau when the artist couldn't travel to each city where he (no female artists back then) was needed, and it worked really well. The file cabinet in the Graphic Unit is stuffed with these composite "hits" along with a memo describing how the work was utilized in the investigation. There was even a folder marked "dead ringers," composites with such a strong likeness that the artist might even be put in for an award or commendation.

As well as this process worked, there still weren't enough artists in the bureau to keep up with the requests. Around 1985, Horace Haefner, the Graphic Unit chief, recognized the need to have more trained artists all around the country and decided that he would be the person to make it happen. He invited several well-known artists from state and federal agencies to a brainstorming session at Quantico, where they huddled for days coming up with a rough syllabus of what the ideal training would look like. The FBI Forensic Facial Imaging Class was born and would be available to anyone in law enforcement who was assigned to be a sketch artist for their agency.

The students would be taught the same interviewing technique used by the FBI agents, and be given copies of the catalog and FD-383 to use just like the FBI artists did. While the crime scene documentation class was five days long, the facial imaging class spanned a full three weeks. That's a long time to be away from your family, stuck on a marine base in the middle of nowhere, but scores of applicants every year didn't blink an eye. They wanted in.

The FBI class was widely considered to be the best forensic art training available, and I can't help but agree. When I attended in 2002, the class covered everything a forensic artist could be expected to encounter in their career: composite sketching, cognitive interviewing techniques, how to create age-progressed images of fugitives, and postmortem identification techniques.

I was a lot luckier than most of the students in my class, because I lived in Maryland and could go home on the weekends. Reid and I had been dating for about six months, and at this point I knew he was pretty special. Here's just one of the many indicators of his awesomeness: I needed to have someone come over and feed my cat Daisy while I was away and debated asking him. I didn't want to be presumptuous, because asking your boyfriend to take care of your cat for three weeks is kind of a big deal. He only lived about a mile from me, so it wasn't really out of his way, but still I hesitated. When I finally got up the nerve to ask, with "you don't have to" already on the tip of my tongue, he got a funny look on his face. *Uh-oh, I've gone too far!* I thought. Then, he said, "Would it be OK if she just stayed at my apartment instead?"

What a guy! I couldn't have asked for anything better, and just hoped it wouldn't upset Daisy to be in a new environment for so long. I shouldn't have worried. Reid told me on the first night she got out of her carrier, walked the circumference of his apartment, then settled on the ottoman for a nap.

Walking through the FBI Academy is like being inside a great big Habitrail. Each building is connected by a series of glass hallways, so it's entirely possible to be there the full three weeks and never step foot outside or feel a drop of rain. If you got lost and didn't want to ask for directions, the worst that would happen was that you'd make a full loop and end up right back where you started.

The class was held in a dank basement classroom of the FBI Academy. Jokes were made about the mold level in the building and the asbestos that had to be in the walls, but nobody was really complaining. Getting into the FBI class was the brass ring for forensic artists around the world.

The first morning started at 8:30 AM with introductions all around, and once again, I was the only bureau employee in a room full of cops. But this time I really felt like I had something to prove. Everyone in the class were already experienced sketch artists, and I had never done a composite drawing in my life. There's a lot more to composite sketching than just being able to draw, and I knew I was going to be judged, not just by fellow students but also by my supervisor. How would it look if the FBI's newest hire couldn't keep up with the rest of the artists?

After the introductions, Gary handed out the FD-383s and pretty much said go. Everyone else in the class got all their supplies out and got started drawing right away, but I was flummoxed. At this point in my career, I barely knew what a composite was. Yes, I had seen them occasionally on the news, but I had no idea how to go about putting one together on the page.

I looked around and saw one person sketching in the head shape and then fitting in the eyes, nose and mouth, and others starting with the individual features and then adding the head shape around it. I looked at the form. *Oh, OK, now I get it.* This was our preinstruction drawing, and the object was to get something on the page so the instructors could see what our drawing level was. We'd find out "the FBI way" when we were done.

Now came the guts of the class—not just learning how to assemble a composite sketch but how to effectively interview a witness. We were taught how to ask questions in a way that frees up the witness to talk as much as they want and phrase them so they can't be answered in one or two words. Instead of "What color were his eyes?" we'll ask, "What can you tell me about his eyes?" Now, we might hear something like, "They were really close together, intense, and so dark they were almost black," rather than a one-word answer like brown.

The next week, we walked into class to find each of us had a plastic skull and block of clay sitting on our desks, and we'd spend the next few days learning what's known as the American (or tissue-depth) method of facial approximation.

First, we needed to get acquainted with facial anatomy. Our instructor had us roll out lengths of clay, and we applied them to the skull, one by one, as she explained where the muscle's origin point was, and where it inserted. For instance, some of the facial muscles connect bone to bone, others originate on the bone and insert into another muscle, and some muscles in the face aren't connected to any part of the skull at all.

This was pretty much a crash course in facial anatomy, because it's impossible to cram all that information into your head in one morning and make it stick. Still, I made up my mind that I wasn't going to have to rely on charts in the future; I would memorize all the bones and muscles of the skull if it killed me. No sooner had we applied all the muscles than it was time to tear them all off again.

We used little white erasers, the kind that come in mechanical pencils, as guides for how much clay to put on the skull. After gluing them to different spots on the skull, we applied strips of clay corresponding to the thickness of the eraser in that area. This was the technical part of the process; fleshing out the empty spots and making it all look like a realistic face was where the artistry came in.

The facial imaging class was like the college life I never had. I'd jump out of bed half an hour before class started, run by the Starbucks kiosk for a mocha, and be able to make it to the classroom with five minutes to spare. Then, it was like being in the best art class all day long.

Every night we hung out at the Boardroom for beer and war stories, and every night the stories would get bigger, louder, and funnier with friendly arguments revolving around skulls, maggots, or how to fingerprint a cadaver. I loved every minute of it.

4

Well, That Escalated Quickly

Most artists in the unit gravitated toward crime scene diagramming and didn't seem to mind that the lion's share of the facial imaging went to a few select artists. This sort of thing isn't limited to the FBI, of course. Supervisors get used to depending on certain employees for certain tasks, so it's natural that they would go to them first. The thing was, I wanted to be one of the go-to people too. I knew I'd have to make it clear that not only was I interested in that kind of work, but I also had the chops to do it.

So, I spoke up. Whenever Gary would talk about a terrific photo retouch that another artist had done, I would wholeheartedly agree, and add, "Next time something like that comes in, and it's not a rush, could I take a stab at it? I'm really interested in this type of work." After enough pestering, I finally got my wish.

I had no idea who Whitey Bulger was when I started at the bureau, but I soon found out. James "Whitey" Bulger Jr. was the boss of the largely Irish American mob in Boston from the 1970s through the '90s. He also happened to be an FBI informant who had been on the lam since 1994, when his FBI handler John Connolly let him know that he was about to be indicted. Not only had Connolly given the FBI's reputation a black eye, but Bulger's ability to evade capture became more embarrassing to the bureau with every passing day. The order had come down from on high: get this guy no matter what it takes.

Most fugitive age progressions are routine five- to ten-year updates to the case file, usually on the anniversary of the crime, but with Bulger it seemed there was a new request every time the wind blew. By 2002 every artist in the unit had done an age progression of him. Now, it was my turn.

This newest request was based off a tip from someone who believed they had seen Bulger, and an artist from the Georgia Bureau of Investigation interviewed the witness to create the image. It was beautifully rendered in charcoal, and there was no reason not to release it, but the agent wanted a photographic version instead.

Now, it really doesn't matter whether an image is done in pencil, pixels, or purple crayon, but what an agent wants, an agent gets, especially if it's Bulger you're talking about. I'm sure Gary pointed this out. But digital photo retouching was still relatively new in 2002, so photorealism was seen as more high-tech and, therefore, "better." All this made a perfect case for Gary to hand over to a new employee, and an opportunity to prove myself. I had years of Photoshop experience under my belt and had certainly retouched enough wrinkles and blemishes out of photos; now I just needed to put some in.

In this case, the changes to Bulger were fairly simple, and I used the same photo the artist in Georgia had based her sketch on. The agent wanted the image turned around as quickly as possible, and I got it to him within a few days. He was happy with the result, and it did the trick with Gary. After that, I was assigned more age-progression cases, and even some postmortem retouches.

I got a surprise a few weeks after I submitted the image to the agent when I was channel surfing one night. I bolted upright and pointed at the TV. "That's my retouch!" I yelped. Thank goodness for TiVo. We rewound it and there it was, a reenactment of two FBI agents passing around my age progression of Bulger. It might have been *48*

Hours or *America's Most Wanted*, I don't remember. But I was thrilled. I have no desire for fame or fortune, but c'mon—it's kind of cool to see something you did appear on TV.

When a mob boss goes on the run with a satchel full of money, you don't expect to find him in a modest two-bedroom apartment in Santa Monica, California. By the time he was arrested, the difference in his appearance was stunning. Even though multiple forensic artists at different agencies had done depictions of Bulger at one time or another, none of us got very close. When Bulger was younger, he had a long, rectangular, chiseled face, and in nearly every photo he was smiling. Given those photographs to work from, and without any other information at our disposal, we all went in the same direction.

I was shocked when I saw his arrest photo. It looked like it had been warped, and I could swear that the width of his head increased by 50 percent. I actually did an overlay in Photoshop to make sure. Yes, of course, his features were all in the same place, but the true width of his head had been disguised by a full head of hair in his youth. Now he was bald, scowling and looking pretty pissed off, unlike all the previous versions of him smiling winningly for the camera.

The image I had done of Bulger wasn't a typical age progression, given that the information I used came from a witness's description. But it showed that I was more than capable of digital imaging and would be able to handle bona fide casework after my probation ended.

———————

After I had a few age progressions under my belt, but no hits, I began wondering whether I was doing it right. I mean, shouldn't somebody have been arrested by now? That's really the only way we can measure our ability as artists. Gary knew as well as anybody that there is a good deal of luck involved with all types of forensic art, especially age progressions. The longer a person has been on the run just increases the likelihood of faded memories, or the possibility that the fugitive had died and is buried somewhere in an unmarked grave. Still, I wanted a hit to prove to everyone (and to myself) that I could do this job.

In the summer of 1983, Sharon Johnson was beaten into unconsciousness at a motel in Harrisonburg, Virginia, and died from her injuries days later. Her boyfriend, Ronald Jerome Jones, was the prime suspect. A witness saw him kicking Johnson while she lay on the floor, enraged because he thought she had stolen five dollars from him.

The most recent photo I had of Jones was over ten years old and was degraded after being scanned and rescanned several times over. If this had been any time after 2010, I would have done the image in Photoshop with a digital stylus. But all I had back then was a mouse, which you can imagine is next to impossible to draw with. I got out the tracing paper and a light box and did a sketch over the original image in pencil.

While any number of things can happen to change a person's looks over the years, there are some things that happen to everyone. Gravity takes effect, and parts of your face that you thought would stay put don't. Fat pads are one of the first things to go, as they loosen and drop from your cheekbones, forming the "parentheses" lines around your mouth. Because the tip of your nose is made up of cartilage, it will head south over the years, and even get larger too, especially if you're a heavy drinker. Earlobes start elongating for the same reason; they're just skin and cartilage, and with no bone to hang on to, they begin to droop.

Just a few little touches are enough to make a face look older—a little puffiness here, some jowls there, and maybe a few forehead lines, crow's feet and soft wrinkles. This is where our knowledge of facial anatomy comes into play. The lines and wrinkles on your face form perpendicular to the way the muscle stretches. Think of it like an elastic waistband. The muscle of your forehead pulls up, vertically, so that means the wrinkles will form horizontally.

Less than two weeks after sending in the finished drawing, I received an email from the agent: "We got him." Jones's case had been featured on *America's Most Wanted* in the "15 Seconds of Shame" segment, and a woman recognized him as someone she had seen wandering in the neighborhood.

I wasn't unleashed on the public after taking the facial imaging class. Because I was a junior hire, it would take a few years until I worked my way up the ladder to doing composites of my own. Until then, I would go on "ride-alongs" with more experienced forensic artists to watch them work.

Most of the composites that were done by the FBI involved an artist jumping on a plane when they were least expecting it. This day, we were only going as far as the second floor of headquarters for the interview, where MATT, a senior artist, would do the drawing via video link.

The only thing I can say about the witness is that he was "a detainee." I'm not being coy; I honestly don't remember where he was from or whom he was describing. It happened over twenty years ago, and I was too new and geeked out to focus.

Imagine being a fly on the wall and you're sitting in a secure and darkened room, inside another secure and darkened room, with video monitors all around while an artist next to you is interviewing someone in an orange jumpsuit thousands of miles away through an interpreter. Yes, it was cool as hell.

It was also where I got an early introduction to one of the many things that can go sideways during a composite interview. When things like that happen, you just have to think on your feet.

I was watching Matt work out the placement and size of the eyes in the drawing. The witness had described big eyes, and that's what

Matt drew. But then the witness says, "bigger." Not to worry, artists want input, and agents always stress to the witness that changes can be made at any time. Matt complied, making the eyes noticeably larger and then held the sketch in front of the camera.

"Bigger." More discussion, more adjustments, and now we've got a sketch of a balding, middle-aged man with huge expressive eyes down on paper. "Bigger," the witness insisted through the interpreter.

"Bigger?" Matt confirmed.

"Yes," said the witness, nodding his head emphatically. "Bigger."

Matt was a seasoned forensic artist and had been doing sketches for years, but I'm sure at the moment he hoped he was experiencing a glitch in the translation matrix, because if he drew those eyes any bigger the suspect was going to start looking like a Precious Moments figurine.

But the first rule of composite art is that you have to draw what the witness wants, and not what you think would look right. Matt tactfully questioned the witness through the interpreter: "Are the eyes bigger this way, up and down?" while gesturing with his hands, or "Were they bigger lengthwise, like this?" Matt was careful to not be argumentative or ask blatantly leading questions, but a drawing isn't going to be useful to anybody if it's clearly anatomically impossible for a person to have eyes the size of golf balls.

But this witness was insistent, and poor Matt ended up with a drawing that he readily admitted was laughable and hoped would never see the light of day. Gary agreed and said, "There's no way we can release this." Again, I had only been in the bureau a few months, so I didn't appreciate the lesson in this until later.

A witness's description of a person is dependent on the conditions and emotions at the time. Lighting, vantage point, mood all play a part in properly seeing and then remembering what a person looked like. When you're terrified and face-to-face with someone who's about to do you harm, it's easy to understand why a person could focus on the eyes and remember them much larger than they actually were. Some witnesses only remember the gun after being mugged, and I can't say I blame them.

Nothing can truly prepare you for your first composite, other than jumping in and doing it. But with hindsight I can see it wouldn't have been the best of situations for even an experienced artist. Typically, composite interviews with witnesses are done in the agency's interview room, which unfortunately is the same room they use when questioning suspects. They are spare, without a speck of decor, no paintings on the walls, no windows. It's just two or three chairs and a table, sometimes with a metal loop on the side for attaching handcuffs.

Because the FBI Laboratory is in a secure facility in the middle of a working military base, trying to bring in any visitor is a logistical nightmare. If we're assisting on a case within driving distance, we'll usually meet the witness at the requesting sheriff's office or police station. Otherwise, we'll go to the local FBI field office, which was the situation here.

Composites generally take two to three hours, so they are normally scheduled in a window either before or after lunch. People can lose interest in helping the police very quickly when their stomach is rumbling or they are worried about picking up their kids from school.

This arrangement was worse: the witness's husband and children had come with her and were going to wait outside the interview room until she was done. I don't have kids, but I sure remember what it was like to be one. Having to sit in an office after being in school all day wasn't going to go well. I worried that the mother was going to hurry through the session to get out as fast as possible.

She had been sitting in her car outside a bank when she noticed a man walking hurriedly across the parking lot. Later, when she heard a robbery had occurred, she realized she had most likely seen the person who had done the crime.

The interview started off well enough, but after about thirty minutes the witness said she had to go—as in, now. All I had at that point was a rough draft, a very generic sketch with little to no shading. Normally this would be the point where we would start making adjustments and refine the drawing. But nope, she was done with the whole thing and wanted to go home. I ended up scribbling in the hair as a last mad dash to get some type of a completed drawing while she was standing up and reaching for her coat and purse.

The whole experience was an embarrassing mess for me, and an extremely stressful experience for the witness and her family. If nothing else, my first composite taught me how it should *not* be done, and looking back, I think I got the worst one of my career out of the way first.

It was the middle of the night and I was stationed in a plain white room at FBI headquarters, prepping to do a remote interview. I was more than a little concerned. The witness was an informant in the ongoing "war on terror," and frankly, I was afraid that he wouldn't speak to me because I was a woman.

Any worries about that evaporated in minutes. He was quite the flirt in his Members Only jacket, joking with the agents next to him, and happily sipping a soda. He spoke English very well, so we didn't need an interpreter, and from the looks of things he was having the time of his life.

In fact, he was having so much fun I wondered if this wasn't just a ruse on his part. If that's what was going on, I seriously doubt the agents would have fallen for it. Maybe this was a double-cross on the agents' parts, and they were playing him. I had no idea at the time, but if I had to guess, I'd say he was making up the whole thing.

False allegations are a fact of life for anyone working in law enforcement, and forensic artists are no exception. Not all witnesses have the best intentions, and they all aren't necessarily telling the truth, either. What they most likely didn't count on is that they would be asked to describe the suspect to a sketch artist. When confronted with this awkward situation, they have two choices: make up a fictitious face or describe one that actually exists.

It's harder than you think to conjure up a believable face out of thin air. Often the witness starts out describing the "suspect" in vague and nebulous terms, which of course ends up as a vague and nebulous-looking composite. But then they start worrying because the drawing is starting to look a bit *too* nondescript. Here's when they may try to jazz things up a bit to keep the artist from getting suspicious. "Oh wait, I didn't mention that he had really huge ears? Yeah, and really bushy eyebrows. They looked like caterpillars!"

It's a lot easier to think up a face that you already know and describe that to an artist instead. It could be a friend, or a neighbor, or even a movie star. *What are the chances this is even going to work?* the person thinks. But when they see the rough sketch, their heart stops. "Wait, did I say his nose was crooked? No, no, it was straighter than that, with a bump on the end. And he had a scar halfway across his face. I can't believe I forgot that!" Now, the witness is backpedaling as fast as they can before the artist realizes she's just created a drawing of Harrison Ford.

What's really infuriating, though, is to be working on a case that's in the news and to hear some yokels making judgments about the victim or saying that they made it all up. Days after interviewing an individual who had been kidnapped and held hostage for months, I turned on the radio to hear two news radio hosts yukking it up:

"C'mon are we really supposed to believe that happened?"

"Yeah, it sure smells phony to me."

"How much you want to bet that the supposed victim ends up with a book deal and a movie of the week?"

Really guys? Wasn't this supposed to be a news show?

Yes, of course the person was telling the truth; several weeks later I got an email that the kidnappers had been rounded up. What about the books, movie deal, magazine covers? All turned down.

We had been taught in the facial imaging class that we had to be prepared to draw anything. Usually, that meant things like tattoos, baseball caps, and clothing, but I'll wager that I got one of the oddest composite sketch assignments of all.

A boy had been abducted when he was five years old, held captive, and assaulted in a dilapidated cabin in the woods. Years later, a suspect was in custody for a string of child sexual assaults, and police had reason to believe that he was the one who had abducted the boy. The problem was, the boy hadn't gotten a good look at his kidnapper, so showing him a lineup wouldn't have been helpful. Added to that was the amount of time that had passed since.

Was there some kind of link that the police hadn't thought of, something to let them know whether they were on the right track? If the victim, by now a young man, recognized a photo of where he had been taken, that would certainly be a start. The problem was that the building had been torn down years before.

Police contacted the landowner to see if he had any photos that might corroborate the boy's description. He didn't, but told police that he could picture it as if he had seen it yesterday.

And that's how I was called in to do a composite sketch of a shack.

Getting a general description of a suspect before we head out to do a composite is always helpful in preparing additional reference material. For instance, the investigator might say that the witness had described a heavyset White male with a facial tattoo and baseball cap. In that case, we'd make sure that we had lots of reference images for tattoos, as well as logos for sports teams.

All anyone knew going in was that it was a single-room shack with a tin roof. This wasn't something that had been built according to a blueprint. It had essentially been slapped together with scraps of wood and layers of cardboard. I brought along sales catalogs from Home Depot, lumber stores, and building contractors, and brushed up on my perspective drawing skills.

The landowner gave me a description just like this was a regular composite, and his memory was remarkable. He described the shape of the winding dirt road that led up to the shack, where it stood in a clearing in the woods. He was very sure that there was one window to the left of the front door, two windows on one side, and a cement stoop with a chunk that had broken off. He described the corrugated tin roof, the smokestack from the coal heater, and even the fake brick-patterned cardboard that was used as siding.

When I was done, the detective took the drawing and went back to meet with the boy in an office down the hall. I was pacing in the room, hoping that I had done well enough, and hoping that if the boy recognized the shack, it could give the investigators some leverage in the case.

About ten minutes later the detective came back into the interview room beaming, and said, "I could hug you." He described how he had shown it to the young man, being careful not to say anything that might prompt him, and heard the words he had been hoping for: "That looks like the place I was taken when I was little."

The detective told me that the drawing gave them even more evidence that they had the right person in their sights, and thanked me for flying halfway across the country to do the sketch. I would have liked to know what happened in the end, but owing to the nature of

the case I wasn't comfortable asking for updates. I had the name of
the landowner but nothing else. The identity of the suspect and the
victim weren't necessary for me to know.

———————————

There was a steep learning curve at the FBI, but not all of that was
related to work.

After being on such a small team at Hopkins, it was a major change
for me to be among so many artists, which made it difficult to get
to know each other. The room setup didn't help; we all worked in
cubicles with six-foot-high walls. I generally got along with everyone,
though rumors and gossip abounded. High school never seems to end.
The navy was the same way, and now the FBI.

I always took it with a grain of salt. But stories about BRENT seemed
to have a common thread. He was always telling jokes with a loud,
booming voice that you could hear coming down the hallway, but
more than one person warned me from firsthand experience that he
had a hot temper and could "get in peoples' faces."

Misunderstandings that would be the plot basis for a sitcom would
turn into something that he'd take great offense at, and then he'd
erupt. One story was that he became irate when someone placed an
interoffice envelope on his desk. "Who the hell was in my cubicle?
Nobody should come into my space! Put it in the mail sorter like
you're supposed to!"

If it happened that way, I'm sure the person who committed the
affront was just trying to be helpful. We often needed to read and
sign interoffice memos, so it made sense to pass the envelope from
cubicle to cubicle instead of going back and forth to the mail bin.

Stories get blown out of proportion all the time, but I made a
mental note to never put so much as a Post-it on his phone. Every
communication would be via email from now on.

Besides, I was never one for office gossip. I've learned that when anybody says something snarky to you about another person, you can bet they are saying snarky things to other people about you. I like to make up my own mind and go by what I see with my own eyes. That's why I was completely unprepared when it came to be my turn, and I learned firsthand what people had been talking about.

I was talking to a coworker in the computer room right outside our unit. It was a small area, only about ten feet by ten feet. The door was always kept locked, even if someone was inside, because the whole point was to keep the area secure. Everyone in the office had a key, though, so if you wanted to come in, you'd tap on the glass, and whoever was inside would give you the thumbs-up to come in.

At one point, Brent came to the window and looked in. I motioned with my thumb toward my coworker while mouthing the words, "You here for me or him?" I started to get up to open the door, but then he left.

A few minutes passed before Brent came back to the window, this time looking agitated. Before I knew it, he had opened the door and was barreling toward me yelling, "Don't you ever do that to me again!"

"What?" I jumped up, surprised. "What? Do what?"

"You know what you did! You don't brush me off and tell me to go away like that, like I'm nothing!" He was barely two feet in front of me, arm outstretched and his finger pointed in my face.

"What?! No, no, no, you misunderstood!" Motioning toward the other coworker, I said, "I was pointing toward him, asking if you wanted to talk to him! I would never do that to you!"

"No, that's not what happened! You were jerking your thumb, like telling me to get out of here! Nobody ever treats me like that! I will *not* be disrespected!"

Now, this is a small room with only one way out, and Brent was smack dab in the middle of it, blocking my exit. Did I mention that Brent also happens to be a very large man? He's got to be at least

275, possibly 300 pounds of solid muscle. I was cornered and freaking out. I thought that at any moment Brent was going to clock me, if not on purpose, then accidentally, because he was waving his arms around as he ranted.

All this was happening in a matter of thirty seconds. Brent was getting himself worked up even more and got to within inches of me. That left an opening in the doorway, and I saw my chance to escape. I ducked under his arm and bolted out the door. Several people had heard all the commotion, and their heads were popped up above their cubicles like meerkats.

I went straight to Ron and Gary, my heart still pounding. They must have heard the racket, because they didn't act too surprised to see me. I wasn't scared anymore; I was royally pissed off. This was the FBI, for Pete's sake! How could this happen here? I never in my life had reason to be afraid at work—not in the navy, not at Hopkins, and not even as a teenager when I worked in a candy store alone at night. There was no way on God's green earth I was going to put up with it here.

Ron and Gary both said something about "taking care of things" but weren't very convincing. I didn't know it then, but at that point the decision was out of their hands. It would be up to the section chief, NORMAN BEAN, in the front office to decide.

"Don't I get to talk to him and tell him what happened?" I asked. "He needs to know what happened before he makes a decision."

"No, don't worry, we'll tell him."

That didn't sit well with me. But I could see the writing on the wall and decided to wait and see what punishment was meted out. At the very least I expected there would be a written reprimand in Brent's file, and possibly a day or two suspension. But Mr. Bean decided differently. As it turned out, all he got was a finger-wag and a verbal warning: *Now, Brent, when you are working at the premier law enforcement agency in the world, you are not allowed to yell at and threaten your coworkers. If you could remember that, that would be great.*

Or something to that effect, I imagine.

I wasn't happy about this one bit, and told Ron that I didn't think it was enough of a punishment. I knew verbal warnings did nothing; if it wasn't in writing, it didn't count. If Brent ever went off the rails again it would be treated as his first offense, and not as a pattern of behavior. But once the section chief decides, that's it.

Theoretically, I could have gone over his head—that's what the chain of command was for—but I thought it would just make things worse, and I'd be seen as the troublemaker. Others in the unit had experienced Brent's wrath too, but apparently I was the first person to insist that upper management get involved. Everyone had always shrugged their shoulders and said, "That's just how Brent is."

It's FBI management's job to ensure that employees are protected from a hostile work environment, so why wasn't anyone willing to speak up? It didn't occur to me at the time that involving the front office would only make things worse.

5

Finding the Missing

"Hey, whatcha doing?" asked Reid. He usually called every morning to make sure I got to the office okay, and to just say hi. "Looking at heads in buckets. You?"

There was a pause. "Well, that's something you don't hear every day."

I couldn't tell him at the time, but I was digitally scrubbing the blood and gore from a photo of failed suicide bombers. They succeeded in killing themselves, but nobody else, thank goodness. In order to keep the heads from drying out and shriveling up, the coroner was keeping them fresh in a bucket of saline, just like flowers last longer if you add a little 7 Up to the water. My job that day was to retouch the photos to make them more suitable for release to the media. The identities of the bombers were still unknown, so the police were turning to the public in the hope of getting useful tips.

I had my work cut out for me. Several things can happen to a body when you strap explosives on it. If the bomber is wearing the device on his chest when it detonates, it's like a Wile E. Coyote cartoon. The facial features go all over the place, teeth can end up where the eyes were, and the nose turns inside out. It's essentially a mess, and they look ridiculous. If they wear the device on their back, like these guys did, the head pops off, taking the spine with it. Then the head becomes a projectile, ricocheting off the walls and banging up the face even more than the explosion did.

If I'm coming across as callous, I don't mean to. It's just . . . I don't feel anything for dead terrorists, and that's what they were. They certainly weren't victims. For victims, I feel all the empathy in the world. But I could completely detach myself from these two.

Besides, I was working under an extremely tight deadline, so there wasn't time for reflection or deep introspective thoughts.

For all the FBI agents knew, these three dead men attempting to blow up a local café could be the first salvo in an orchestrated, multitiered attack. Who knew if there were more, or where'd they strike next?

"Can you get all three of them back to us in a day or two?" the agent asked.

"Absolutely," I said. Normally, this is a ridiculous turnaround for your typical postmortem retouch, but this situation was anything but typical. There were multiple agencies working to identify these guys, which led to a bit of healthy competition. Agents don't want excuses, so you just work like hell to accommodate them, even if there's not enough time to make it perfect.

I worked a few hours that night on all three, came in early the next day, and had them back to the agent within thirty-six hours from the time I got them. I told him they may not be as pristine as they could have been if there were more time. But these weren't going to be inspected with a fine-toothed comb, they were to be put out on the street to see if they might look familiar to anyone.

It was great to see the bombers identified a few days later. I was happy with the resemblance for two of them, not so much with the third. But, then again, the only thing holding his head together was his flesh. His skull was shattered, like a bag of marbles that would change shape depending on how you held it. As I said, this wasn't a typical case of unidentified remains.

So, what is typical? How are these cases solved in the United States, and how many are there? There's tons of technology around to identify people, so there can't be very many. Right?

Here's something to think about: You go out to the store one day, but don't come back. Years later and several hundred miles away, kids are playing near a stream when they stumble across something funny-looking. After a bit of digging and poking around, a skull rolls out. Your skull. Police are called, and the area is cordoned off to protect the already-disturbed crime scene.

The grim task of finding all the pieces that are left of you begins. Some of your hair might be up in a bird's nest, maybe a few teeth have fallen out and are at the bottom of the river. Whatever parts of you that haven't been eaten or carried off by scavengers will be collected and documented.

Now the medical examiner is trying to figure out who you are, and the police are curious, too, because it looks like it's a homicide. If they don't know who you are, they have no way to begin figuring out who killed you. Sure, there's missing person records, but after so many years have passed, it's impossible to narrow the results down from the thousands of similar cases.

Your partially decomposed body is laid out on the table, photographed, and documented. The medical examiner was able to pull several fingerprints, but no hits come up because you've never been fingerprinted in your life. Tissue or bone samples are collected for DNA testing, and the results are uploaded to the FBI's National Missing Persons DNA Database. No hits come up there either, because nobody reported you missing.

Maybe it's because you travel all the time and you were never good at keeping in touch anyway. Maybe your parents kicked you out of the house, or maybe you ran away because there was abuse or alcoholism in the home. Or maybe *you* were the toxic member of the family, so nobody was very motivated to find you. What it all boils down to is that the investigators have done everything they can to identify you, but they'll never be able to unless correlating information from you is in a database that can be matched to your remains.

After a year or more, the investigator might ask for a facial approximation, and that's when your skull could end up on my desk. After I'm done, I send everything back to the investigator, and the images are uploaded into NamUs, the National Missing and Unidentified Person System. NamUs is a public, government website containing unidentified remains and missing persons cases.

The idea is that if a family member believes you may be among the unidentified deceased, they can search the gallery of facial approximations within NamUs and see if they might recognize you. And this would be a good thing, except NamUs doesn't work the way it's supposed to.

NamUs wasn't originally developed or funded by the government. It started as a private database created by medical examiners to keep track of their unidentified cases, using off-the-shelf software. It was a noble effort, but medical examiners are not programmers or designers. The interface was decidedly non-user-friendly, the search functions were clumsy to the point of being unusable, and the case details were filled with medical jargon.

In 2007 the National Institute of Justice repackaged the website as NamUs, spending roughly $5 million a year ($67 million to date) to maintain it through various contractors. Here's the problem: the software and interface never changed. It wasn't reverse engineered to factor in the information that the family will logically use to search by.

Fields like "date and location remains found" make sense for medical examiners when they're looking for one of their cases, but it doesn't make sense for anyone else. If your family knew when and where your body was found, they wouldn't be looking in the first place. Data fields like "details of recovery" (putrefied, mummified, insect activity present) and "body parts recovered" (torso missing, hands not recovered, etc.) aren't just useless to the family; they're pretty unsettling as well. The literalness of the data is a further stumbling block to developing matches. Your family knows you weighed 130 pounds, but they aren't going to be able to find you, because according to NamUs you are 10 pounds—the weight of your skeleton.

When you went to the store that day on January 1, 1990, you were twenty years old. Your body was found later in 2000. But when did you actually die? Were you murdered on January 2, 1990? Or sometime later? This matters. Just because you went missing one day doesn't mean you are dead the next. You could have lived twenty more years, changed your hair color, gained a few pounds, and lost a few teeth. And because NamUs isn't a "thinking" algorithm-based system that can calculate those variables, it will be virtually impossible for your family to find you, because NamUs can't do the basic math and return viable matches.

One aspect of NamUs that is especially horrifying to me is the inclusion of graphic, unretouched morgue photos. When your family has accepted the possibility that you might be deceased, do you want them to see what you look like after being beaten and strangled, learning that you died "while urinating in a field" and were found "putrefied and maggot-infested" next to a river? Given those possibilities, it's likely that they won't look at all.

I had a case exactly like this, and the image was awful. Parts of his face were peeling away, his mouth was slack and full of maggots, and his nose partially eaten away by rats. I really would have preferred to have done a facial approximation. That way I could see his facial structure better, and could add things I could discern from the photo, like his goatee and hairstyle. But there was no way the medical examiner was going to remove the head and clean it. The detective asked, and had gotten an emphatic no. I nonetheless did a drawing from this image, thinking it would be a miracle if he were ever identified.

For years, that case haunted me. Should I have done it, should I have told the detective it might do more harm than good? After I retired, I decided to look it up, and was floored to see that he had been identified. I was even more shocked when I saw his photo. Wow, the resemblance . . . it was there, no doubt about it. Thank goodness I hadn't turned that one away, because it actually had worked and gotten him identified. But what I won't do is release his identity, and risk having his family know what a hideous death he suffered.

Maybe you think, *I'll be dead, so I don't care*, but that doesn't mean others feel the same way. Even in death, or maybe I should say, *especially in death*, people deserve dignity.

I see one last problem with NamUs that might be filed under the hashtag "unpopular opinions": *It doesn't make any sense for long-term missing person cases to be on a publicly accessible government website.*

Before anyone gets their dander up, let's look at this logically. One day on NamUs you see the profile for Mary Smith, a twenty-five-year-old Caucasian female, who has been missing from Maryland since 2019.

A few days later you think you see her in the checkout aisle of a supermarket in Florida. You pull up NamUs on your phone to double-check, and yes, it sure does look like Mary. She even has the same kind of tattoo on her wrist. What do you do? Go up and say, "Hi, is your name Mary Smith, and are you from Maryland?" If she says yes, what do you do then, tell her that she's missing? That would sound pretty stupid.

You could call the police, but why? She's just standing there minding her own business. Even if the police did show up and "asked for her papers" to confirm her identity, they can't exactly make her go back to Maryland. The best they can do is tell her family that they have made contact, because Mary Smith has rights, and for all you know the reason she left is because of a hellish home life, and she has no intention of going back.

Of course, it would be completely different if Mary were in some sort of imminent danger, like the girls who were rescued in Ohio after being held hostage by Ariel Castro. In that case, it shouldn't matter who you thought she was, you'd help because you are a good person.

I know *Sleeping with the Enemy* with Julia Roberts is only a movie, but how would you like it if you left an abusive husband and tried to start your life over only to have your image splattered on missing person websites with scores of Internet detectives trying to track you down? Maybe that's what's going on with Mary Smith, and she deserves to be left alone.

6

Obsession

I don't like slasher movies. I didn't like them before I started at the FBI, and I like them even less now. I especially can't tolerate the ones where someone is serenely knitting or watching TV, oblivious that the bad guy is already down in the basement cutting the phone lines. This mode of thinking is why I had to explain to Reid that, whenever he traveled, I'd sleep on the couch with a knife under the cushion instead of in the bedroom upstairs.

"If somebody's going to break into this house, I want to know it and have a fighting chance. If I'm upstairs sound asleep, I won't hear the glass breaking in the living room."

I've always been hyperaware of potential danger. First, because I'm a woman. While I know that I am perfectly able to walk down a dark road looking for a service station if my car runs out of gas, I also know it's not the wisest thing to do.

And second, I realized how vulnerable I was after my apartment was broken into while I was working for the navy in Spain. I was twenty-two years old and lived in a two-bedroom duplex near the beach. It was a quiet, working-class neighborhood, with nothing much going on in the way of crime. If anything, there were burglaries, and we were warned by the base commander that being a "rich American" might make us more of a target.

I was coming home from a midnight shift, and just as I was putting the key in the lock, I had the oddest sensation. I shook it off and then walked inside to find my apartment had been virtually destroyed. In boot camp, this would be called a "hurricane." This is when the company commander decides that her recruits need to learn a lesson in teamwork, so everything in the barracks that isn't nailed down or bolted to the floor is strewn everywhere. That would've been awful enough, but this was far worse. I'll never forget what my formally safe, cute, comfy apartment looked like after the burglars had gotten done with it, and how personally invaded I felt.

Everything I owned was everywhere. Chairs were tipped over, cushions were off the couch, curtains had been torn off the rods, kitchen cabinets had been flung open, and my dishes lay broken on the countertops. Most of my food had been taken too, except for the carton of ice cream melting on the floor. A friend suggested they were looking for money or jewelry hidden inside the Breyers mint chocolate chip. Ha! I had nothing worthy of stealing, not even a radio or a cassette player.

But that wasn't the worst part. I walked into my bedroom to survey the damage. My mattress was on the floor, the sheets had been torn off the bed, dresser drawers were open and empty, and shattered glass was on the floor. I looked out the broken window into the yard, and there, plain as day, was an axe.

They had broken the window with the axe, had a child or very skinny burglar shimmy between the bars, and then opened the front door to let all the other burglars in to help themselves to my stuff! If I had been home when that happened . . . well, I don't even want to think of it.

Since then, I have always had a home security system, even when I lived in a top-floor apartment, because I know that bad guys don't always think logically, and somebody just might want the challenge of shimmying up three balcony railings instead of hitting a ground-floor apartment like an amateur.

I know that security alarms aren't foolproof, and people who are looking to do harm to others aren't thinking logically. But now, instead of reading about these things in the news, I was seeing the reality of them, the aftereffects, the part that the media doesn't show or that wouldn't have the effect on me if they did. Besides looking at bloody crime scene photos, I was interviewing survivors of sexual assault—real people, real women crying three feet away from me as I sat there helplessly, knowing that whatever I said couldn't possibly heal the grief and distress.

While I'd had enough success with composites to feel that I was capable of doing them, I wasn't all that comfortable. I didn't look forward to the assignments like other artists did, and I worried what this meant. Was I really cut out to be a forensic artist?

I talked to Reid about it every so often, and one time he said something quite daring: "You know you're a perfectionist, right? When you feel like you don't have time to really think about things, look at all the different options, and examine everything a few times over, you can sort of freak out a little."

He looked at me to make sure I wasn't freaking out in that very moment. I wasn't. At least not on the outside.

Then he pointed out something I had never thought about before. "You always told me that in the navy you didn't like doing live translating, but you loved transcription. So that's kind of the same thing, in a way, isn't it?"

Now, the wheels in my head were turning. Back when I was a Russian linguist, there were two types of work we did. One was like being a regular in-person interpreter, essentially writing down rough notes of what you were hearing, in Russian, as you heard it. The other type was doing a detailed, line-by-line transcription, and the kind I infinitely preferred. I'd take the rough notes, the reel-to-reel tape of the conversation, and go over every word and syllable until I had it exactly right.

There was a rhythm to the work: left hand on the reel to slow it down, eyes closed to concentrate, right hand pressing the earphones to my head to block out all other noise, both feet alternating on the foot pedals to backtrack and hear it over and over and over again. Sometimes I could hear things clear as a bell; other times it sounded like people talking with a mouthful of taffy. But if I was patient enough and put the words in context with the parts that were garbled, it would start to fit together. It was like a puzzle, and the eight-hour shifts flew by.

Maybe that's why I loved working on skulls so much. Those were like puzzles too: Why is one nostril higher than the other? Why does one corner of the eye turn down when the other doesn't? Why do some people have dimples, and is that something I could predict from their skull?

Figuring this out was a revelation for me. I still practiced composites regularly. I could be called at any moment to do a sketch, and I wasn't about to point to somebody else and say, "Make them go instead." But I could detach myself from using composites as a measuring stick for being an artist and instead focus on what my strengths were, and what I really cared about: facial approximation from skulls.

———————

It's now accepted as fact that faces aren't symmetrical. It's one thing to know that logically in your head and another to try to figure out what to use as a baseline in three dimensions. In Hollywood it's said that certain actors insist on being filmed "from their best side," but that's very two-dimensional thinking.

If you stare at yourself in the mirror or take a photo of yourself, you might notice that your left eye is higher than the right. It also looks a bit smaller. Huh. Is that because your left eye is deeper set than the right, or is your left eyeball itself smaller? Or maybe, your eyeballs are the exact same size, but the orbit, the bony opening that your eyeball sits in, is actually smaller. A person could drive themselves crazy with these types of questions, and by "person," I mean me.

Thoughts like that literally kept me up at night. I wanted to figure out all that could be gleaned from the skull, so I could make my approximations as accurate as possible. Reid could always tell when I had a new skull that was giving me trouble. We might be sitting on the couch talking when he'd notice my gaze veering off and say, "You're looking at my skull again, aren't you?"

Caught red-handed, I had to admit, "Yes, sweetie, but I was listening too!"

This obsession is what led to the Body Farm project. I'm sure lots of people want to get inside those gates for ghoulish reasons, but not me. I wanted answers. The smell, the flies, the maggots were just something I'd have to deal with, which is saying something for a person who is grossed out by a rare steak.

It took months of planning to figure out what I'd need. Getting a team together was the first priority. Wade was a no-brainer, since he was a subject matter expert in facial approximation. I knew the information I wanted to collect, but having another forensic artist to bounce ideas off of was crucial. He had experience in 3D processing too, which was a major plus, because it would take two people to handle the scanning. Who else could I tap?

Kirk was arguably the best model builder in the unit, and the recognized expert in 3D printing before it was a thing. At one point the laboratory director, without one iota of the expertise to make such a judgment, thought the 3D program should be shut down. After news of a 3D printed gun was splashed on the front pages of several newspapers, he had a sudden change of heart, and Kirk's work area became a favorite on his VIP tours.

Since both of our units were large and on different floors, we hadn't ever really met or had a conversation. He had a degree in model making and was a master craftsman at it, the kind of guy who sands the underside of dresser drawers. I went downstairs to introduce myself, tell him about the project, and see if he would be willing to work on the scanning.

I was explaining how forensic artists needed more examples of real skulls to make our facial approximations better, and that I had this great idea to go to the Body Farm to get them and, oh my God, it's going to be so cool because they have donors and life photos so we can use that to study and then to teach classes and what we learned with other artists.

I was rattling on, explaining it with my hands like I do when I get excited, and then I noticed him giving me an odd look, with his head kind of cocked like the dog in the old Victrola ads.

"Is something wrong?" I asked.

"No. I'm just not used to seeing people around here so excited about work."

I knew we'd be friends. He had heard the same things I had when I was brand new to the FBI: "Yeah, you're enthusiastic now, but just wait. You'll get federalized like everyone else." Did people take it as a point of pride that they would eventually turn into government drones? Maybe they were bored with their job, but that wasn't about to happen to me.

I was thrilled that Kirk was on board, because I wanted to work with like-minded people. We had a lot of work to get done in a very short amount of time, and there was no room for wet blankets or people who were looking to kill time. I wanted to get shit done.

Now I needed a photographer. Most forensic artists outside the FBI have to do their own photography for 2D approximations, but there's no reason for that when you have experts on hand. I went to the Photo Unit hoping to snag Geoff. He had photographed plenty of skulls for my casework before, so we already had our workflow down pat. He's a fun person to be around, he's a perfectionist, and he's very patient, something which would be sorely needed for this kind of work.

We would be taking two sets of photographs of each skull. The first would be of the skull alone. Then Geoff would be on standby mode while I grabbed the glue gun and attached all the tissue-depth markers. *Click, click, click,* one skull down, then the process would start all over again.

Now I had to figure out a way to hold the skulls for photography. When you only need to take pictures of one skull, it's OK to take twenty minutes fussing over the alignment while the skull sits on a turntable. But if we wanted to get through ten skulls on our first trip, we'd have to figure out something more efficient that would work on an assembly line.

Each skull needed to be precisely oriented on something called the Frankfort horizontal plane, an anthropological standard that approximates the natural position of the head in life. On the skull, this means that the top part of the external auditory meatus—the bony opening of the ear—will fall into a horizontal line with the bottom of the eye orbit.

This is an extremely important step. If the skull is tilted at even the slightest angle, it could appear to be an entirely different shape than it really is. The Frankfort also provides a common point of reference in research articles, and instruction for the facial approximation process. For instance, when we are following guidelines for predicting facial features, the study will generally have been conducted by aligning the skull in the Frankfort. We need to have the skull aligned the same way; otherwise our measurements, and the results, are going to be off.

What I needed now was a universal skull holder, and that's not something you can just grab at Home Depot. Kirk loves nothing more than a construction problem that needs solving, so I explained the issue. Every skull is different, and so is each foramen magnum, the opening in the base of your skull that your spinal cord passes through. We needed a device that would work on every size and shape of foramen, but there couldn't be any metal, clamps, nuts, or bolts touching the skull. We needed to leave each skull in the exact same condition as it was when we arrived. One scratch on a mandible could blow the deal.

Last, we had to have some kind of rotating stand to attach each skull to, and it had to be calibrated so I could make sure every shot of every skull was set to the same angle as the other. "And I want to be able to change the height. Plus, a level would be nice too, if you can do it!"

"You don't want much," Kirk said drily, but I knew he wasn't really complaining.

He ended up fashioning a device out of multitiered plexiglass rings with rubber-coated nuts and bolts, set on a camera tripod. We tested it out before going on travel, and it worked like a champ. High-five!

Now I had to figure out a way to keep track of what skulls were being photographed, and where they were in the queue to be scanned. The Body Farm has its own numbering system, but we couldn't use its reference numbers, because we had to ensure that others wouldn't accidentally figure out the person's identity. We could have a person's skull, their photographs, their biological information, but not their name. The skulls would start from 001 and go up, and the numbers would be taped onto both the cranium and mandible. The anthropology department would have the cross-reference to their collection on file.

I fiddled around with a few software programs, but in the end analog was best. I made up a chart and kept track of everything with good old pencil and paper. Then came a master inventory, itemizing everything we'd need and where each item would be packed. Inside each container was a checklist, so we'd check and double-check each one before hitting the road.

Nothing like this had been done before, so we had to imagine what the process would be like and go from there. By our second trip we knew to pack lots of Advil. Wade and Kirk took turns scanning, which meant standing on their feet all day holding an unwieldy 3D scanner trying to catch every angle of the skull. Geoff and I had our own pains, him sitting in a cramped corner taking photos all day, and me getting up and down on a linoleum floor putting skulls on a tripod.

The A-team was assembled, and the big day finally came. Wade, Kirk, Geoff, and I met in the garage at the laboratory on a Sunday morning, feeling like kids going on a road trip. We had loaded all the equipment in a bureau van the previous Friday. After a stop at Dunkin' Donuts outside the gates of the marine base, we were on our way. Nine hours later, we pulled up to the gates of Neyland Stadium.

The collection was housed in the basement of the stadium, using old dorm rooms that the football team had lived in. As the collection grew, a wall would be knocked down to make room for more skulls. In the hallway we were immediately hit with the smell of mothballs. Mice could be a problem, and the mothballs were to keep them from nibbling on any of the remains. Hundreds of long cardboard boxes were stacked floor-to-ceiling on metal shelving, and charts were on the walls with instructions of how each skeleton was to be placed within.

Wade and I made a beeline for the skulls that were set out for us, all lined up in neat rows on the table. It's hard to explain what I was feeling at that moment. I had never seen so many skulls in one place, and with so much variation.

"Holy cow, look at this occipital ridge!"

"Whoa! And check out the gonial flaring on this one!"

Kirk and Geoff waited patiently by the door as we marveled, but soon realized we could have stayed there for hours geeking out.

"C'mon guys, you'll have plenty of time to look at skulls later. Let's get some dinner."

After a few hours getting everything unpacked the next morning, we were off to the races. For efficiency's sake, Geoff and I would be in one room photographing one group of skulls while Wade and Kirk were in the other. Kirk would scan a cranium and then hand off the data to Wade. While Kirk was scanning the mandible, Wade would start processing the raw skull data to make sure every angle was captured. It starts off as a "point cloud" of dots—measurements in digital space that need to be converted into a model that a 3D printer is capable of recognizing.

I used a carpenter's level on a tripod, and would aim the laser while adjusting the position of the skull. When I could rotate the skull while still keeping the laser correctly on the Frankfort, I knew it was oriented correctly. On the second day I came across a skull that I could not get oriented correctly no matter how hard I tried. I would get the eyes level only to notice one of the ears was off. I'd fix that, but then I'd notice the other ear was off. I was ready to pull my hair out, then decided to cave in and look at the man's life photo. My jaw dropped when I saw his face. Thank goodness it was a perfectly posed front view, so I could pull over the digital rulers in Photoshop and do some measuring.

I went back to the skull, pointed the laser at it, and there it was plain as day: the left orbit was higher, and more recessed. Maybe that should have been obvious to me from the start, but it's one of those things that forensic artists hadn't been able to predict, or prove for sure. Was the asymmetry of a person's face because of differences in the thickness of the flesh in certain parts, or did it originate in the skull?

Wade had always teased me because I would rip out prosthetic eyeballs on some of my sculptures and redo them if I thought they didn't look right. "Maybe that's how they're supposed to look," he'd say. "You know if you redo them, they're just going to end up the same way." And, yes, they always did.

I had been struggling to fix crooked eyes on certain sculptures, only to find out from the collection that they weren't necessarily meant to be straight. If anyone dared criticizing my work by saying, "His eyes aren't even," I could fire back at them with full confidence, "I know. That's how they are supposed to be."

If we could learn this much from the collection, how much more was there to find out? Could we predict cleft chins, or dimples? Dimples are caused by a defect in the muscle; it splits and that's what causes the indentation. But was the defect of the muscle caused by something on the skull? Or did it just happen? Was there a way to tell the difference between average eyes like Tom Hanks or Jennifer Aniston, or whether they'd be larger and deeply hooded like Steve Buscemi or Lady Gaga?

For so long, artists had been operating in the dark, following outdated guidelines without even knowing it, and doing their best to imagine what any given feature might look like because they didn't have anything concrete to refer to. While a reference collection might not provide every answer to every question, it would be a lot more than artists had now. And at this point, we had only scratched the surface of what there was to learn.

———————

Facial approximation can be a pretty controversial topic around some forensic anthropologists, who point to the number of studies proving that the process doesn't work. What they may not have taken into account is that those studies are inherently flawed because it's impossible to replicate the circumstances of how identifications are actually made, and ignore the reason they can (and do) work in the real world.

In the studies, volunteers were given photos of facial approximations and photos of faces. Their assignment was to correctly match up the approximation with the photo of the corresponding individual. When they only got it right half the time, researchers concluded that facial approximations don't work any better than pure chance. But this doesn't prove that facial approximations don't work, it just proves they don't work well *when the viewer is a stranger.*

If it were possible to create a study where the volunteers were family members of the people depicted in the facial approximations, it would be a completely different ball game. And the reason I know this is because there are countless cases where that's exactly what happened. Maybe it was just "something about the eyes" or a face shape that seemed familiar, but that's all that matters.

It's rare that a complete stranger will be able to correctly match an approximation to a photo of a missing person. Not that they don't try. Cyberslueths attempt to match the fourteen thousand unidentified remains cases with the twenty-one thousand missing persons in the NamUs database and believe with enough time and effort they will be able to find a match, so they can call in a tip to law enforcement. Their hearts are in the right place, but the police know something they don't. There aren't just twenty-one thousand missing person cases in the United States; there are almost ninety thousand. The chances of a person being able to make a correct match without access to 75 percent of the records is very slim.

Another factor that reduces the chances even more drastically is that those ninety thousand cases aren't static. That's because thousands of police agencies from across the United States enter more than six hundred thousand missing person cases into the FBI's missing person file of the National Criminal Information Center each year. A case from Florida is entered, a case from Idaho is removed, a case from Utah goes in, a case from New Jersey goes out. The database is almost a living, breathing thing; it is in constant movement and continuously changing.

When cyndersleuths believe they have a match, they can also be discouraged or even angry when their tips to law enforcement aren't taken seriously. But what are police supposed to do? Knock on a person's door and say, "Somebody on the Internet thinks they found your dead sister, may we please have your DNA for comparison?"

But if police get a call from a person who says, "I saw a facial approximation online, and I think it might be my sister"? Well, now they've got the police's full, undivided attention. And now they are able to ask for a DNA sample for comparison, because a potential relative has come forward.

Most people are fascinated by skulls, and I'd be lying if I said I were any different. No two are alike. I used to think they were, until I got into this line of work. Few people have the opportunity to see even one skull in their lifetime, so there are no words for the first time I stood in a room with twenty skulls lined up in a row. All imaginable shapes, all imaginable sizes, as different from each other as snowflakes.

And that, right there, is the key to facial approximation. The reason we each look like the individual we are is because of the shape and structure of our skull. Your skull is like an armature for the muscles, fat, and flesh that is draped on top of it. If you have wide-set eyes, it's because your eye orbits are widely spaced on your skull. Square jaw? Square mandible. Wide nose? Wide nasal aperture.

Whenever I give a talk about this topic, someone will invariably ask, "How do you know what the person is going to look like?" The thing is, I don't. No forensic artist ever knows for sure. We do the best we can with the information that is available. Our hope is that there will be enough of a resemblance for someone to stop and pay attention long enough to think, *Hey, that might be my cousin Clara I haven't seen in ten years.*

Sometimes we get identifications and are startled by how close the likeness to the missing person is. Other times, we wonder how it ever worked at all. Even just having a picture to go with an article can do the trick, because people have short attention spans. That's why Facebook added those multicolored backgrounds for people to voice their opinion or wish someone a happy birthday. It's an attention-getter.

The FBI does a whole lot of things right, and one of those is the facial approximation process. It's a team effort, and it starts before the skull ever makes it to the forensic artist's desk. The medical examiner is usually the first professional called after the police are notified that a body (or parts of it) has been found. By their very job description, medical examiners deal with human remains that are still "fleshed."

If entirely skeletal remains are received, the medical examiner will generally defer to the forensic anthropologist. They may not always be the first on the scene (there aren't as many forensic anthropologists as there are medical examiners), but for skeletal remains they should always be part of the process.

The investigator in unidentified remains cases might be a police investigator, but he could also be an investigator within the medical examiner's office. It all depends on the state and the agencies as to how this is handled.

And then there is the forensic artist. Generally, it's up to the artist to decide which method will be used for the approximation: a 3D sculpture or 2D drawing. Since both methods use the same guidelines and protocols, they are generally equal in creating an approximation. What matters more than the method used is the skill level of the artists and whether they've been properly trained and have stayed up to date with the most current research on the subject.

Facial approximation has often been referred to as a "blend of art and science," and you can say that's true when it's done right. What do I consider to be "right"?

First, the person attempting to create a sculpture must have intermediate to advanced drawing and sculpting skills. To paraphrase Emerson, "Every artist was once an amateur, but an amateur has no business getting anywhere near a skull." This is the last chance for a person to be identified, so if someone doesn't have the skills to do a facial approximation justice, they should step aside and let a more skilled artist do the work. After all, there will still be plenty of unidentified skulls to go around later.

I once took a workshop on the Manchester method of facial approximation. It started the same way as what I learned in the FBI class: we were each given a copy of a skull along with some of the basic anthropological information, and armed with glue guns and ten pounds of clay, we began attaching tissue depth markers on the face. But instead of applying strips of clay between all the markers, we sculpted in all the muscles of the face.

This is where I started scratching my head. How was I supposed to know the thickness of the orbicularis oculi (eye muscle)? Was it the same all around, or did it taper in parts? What about the other sphincter muscle of the face, the orbicularis oris? Why weren't we adding all the deeper muscles of the face underneath the superficial ones? What about nerves, glands, fat deposits? I soldiered on doing the best I could, following the instructor, while peeking at the work of the other artists in the room.

Once all the muscles were applied and I stood back from my work, I could see how the skull had taken on a bit of life, and a real face was beginning to emerge. But we weren't done yet.

Next, we each made a big round of clay, spread it out like a pizza crust, and draped it over the entire face. This was to simulate the skin layer. If the tissue depth markers poked through, then we were supposed to add additional clay to build up the surface to the depth of the markers.

But then the wheels in my brain turned again, and I wondered, *Why did we go to all the trouble of sculpting the muscles if we were just going to follow the tissue-depth markers in the end?* The only difference I could see between this method and the tissue depth was that there was a lot of time and effort spent on something that hadn't really affected the outcome. The end result of the sculpture was still based on the tissue depth markers.

Now, I'm not about to argue with an anatomist, who knows from firsthand experience the thickness and ranges of variation of the muscles in the face and has more experience, degrees, and knowledge than I could ever have. But there was a good reason for my head scratching, and it explains why most forensic artists don't use this technique in the field: it is extremely time-consuming.

Plus, even though we have the same basic facial anatomy, we all don't look the same under the skin. It's not like an anatomical drawing, where everything is neat and orderly with clear delineation between muscle groups. The human face is a tangle of muscles, tendons, nerves, glands, and fat cells. Plus, there are anatomical aberrations to consider.

You might have heard the expression, *"It takes forty-three muscles to frown, but only seventeen to smile."* Scientists don't agree on how many muscles it actually takes, but it doesn't matter, because not everyone is born with the same number of facial muscles. The risorius, one of the smiling muscles located on the corner on either side of the mouth, isn't present in all people. Some have it, some don't.

I knew enough to keep my mouth shut, but I didn't stop thinking about it or questioning approximation methods and guidelines. That's not just the way my brain works; it's how science works too.

I hunted down every research paper I could find, studying the most current, scientifically based approximation techniques. I picked the brains of the anthropologists and asked them to explain some of the more complex verbiage. When I realized that the guidelines that were taught in the FBI facial imaging class had become outdated, I decided I should share all the new data with other forensic artists. I got permission from the FBI's Office of Integrity and Compliance to start a website about forensic art and began posting articles and diagrams explaining what I had learned.

They say no good deed goes unpunished, and unfortunately, I found out how true that is.

7

The Upside Down

A lot happened all at once in the summer of 2009. First, Gary retired. Then a reorganization was announced. Wade and I, along with three other artists, would be transferred to the Photo Unit. In exchange, an equal number of photographers would move to the Graphic Unit. An investigation, courtesy of the inspector general's office, was in full swing, and RANDALL BOGGS, one of the artists in the unit, seemingly disappeared into thin air.

There were no warning signs; we all arrived at work one day to find that his entire cubicle had been cleaned out. Everything was gone—the desktop computer, laptop, books, scraps of paper, everything. Even at the FBI, having a colleague's work area vanish without warning is pretty unusual. Ron and Gary wouldn't tell us what was going on until we practically mutinied. Was he sick? Was he in trouble? Was he fired? Was one of us next?

"No, no, no, and no" they said, "Don't be dramatic. He's been transferred to a field office temporarily for, um, health reasons."

I don't know if anyone else in the unit bought that, but I immediately thought, *Bullshit*. The reason for my skepticism was because I had been summoned to the inspector general's office to give a statement about an incident that had occurred a year earlier. I had gone into the computer room looking for the external hard drive backup that was dedicated to the Body Farm project, but it wasn't there. That's when a coworker volunteered, "Oh, I saw Randall walk out with it." Steam practically shot from my ears.

To put it kindly, Randall was one of the more abrasive individuals in the unit. He was pompous and condescending to coworkers, smarmy and obsequious to supervisors, and had a passing relationship with the truth. Every workplace has a Randall, and the FBI is no exception. During my first month at the bureau, he made a point of insulting me in front of the unit when I asked him a question about crime scene diagramming: "I'll try to explain it to you, even though you won't be able to understand."

Randall hadn't asked for the hard drive, and he knew good and well that I wouldn't have given it to him anyway. According to the terms of the Body Farm agreement, the only people allowed access to the data while the project was ongoing were the people directly involved in it. That would be me—because I had created the project and was the designated "stakeholder"—then Wade, the photographer Geoff, the modelmaker Kirk, and the contract specialist who makes sure all the rules are followed.

Everything related to the project was on that hard drive: skull scans, life photos, the donor's medical background, anthropological workup, and more. This was "personally identifiable information," and there are very strict rules governing this type of material. Before the Body Farm project could be approved, it first had to be vetted by an internal review board to ensure that any personal information about the donors would be protected.

Randall had a research project of his own, a software that would, ostensibly, create digital facial approximations automatically. Millions of dollars had been spent on it, but the results were less than impressive. No matter how different each skull was, the results came out looking almost identical to each other. The software didn't allow for hair or eyes, so they all resembled bald, orange, sleeping mannequins.

My worry, beyond the fact that he had taken information that didn't belong to him, was that he would use the Body Farm data for his software.

Just like every other person in the unit, I had a number of unpleasant dealings with Randall over the years. I knew he'd be a jerk if I went to him and asked what the hell he thought he was doing with research material that didn't belong to him, so I went to Gary.

"He's got a clearance. What's the problem?"

I liked Gary as a supervisor, but Randall was his blind spot. He spoke often of his "genius," and in his eyes Randall could do no wrong. I tried to get it through to Gary that what he had done was a clear violation of the project agreement, but Gary kept saying, "He's got a clearance. What's the big deal?"

I was irritated beyond words that I couldn't get through to him. "Gary, this is different. It's a government contract with an outside vendor. Security clearances have nothing to do with it." But the harder I tried to explain it, the more Gary waved my concerns away.

Still, since I knew about the violation, I was duty-bound to report it to the contract officer, and I wasn't looking forward to it. I have never seen a person so enraged. He was absolutely livid, incredulous as to Randall's audacity and not about to let him get away with it.

After that, everything that happened was far above my pay grade, and the shrapnel started flying. My interview at the inspector's office took the whole day, and it's a very unsettling experience. Even though I knew I wasn't the subject of the investigation, I was sternly reminded that could change, depending on what came to light. The last question I was asked was, "Do you have any evidence to back up the statements you've made?" Well, yes, I did.

I'm notorious for not cleaning out my email regularly, so I still had all the emails between me and Randall battling out the return of the hard drive, replete with his snarky responses that I wasn't the boss of him. I got the hard drive back, eventually. But what do you think the odds are that Randall actually wiped copies of the stolen files from his hard drive, like he was supposed to?

One thing I was sure of, the reorganization had absolutely nothing to do with Brent, or management's feigned concern about keeping me safe from another one of his outbursts.

He would come up to the Graphic Unit several times a week, when he seemingly had no business being there; his work area was downstairs in the model shop. He made a point of hanging out at a friend's desk most of the time, which was an arm's swing away from me. I went to Gary several times asking him to limit Brent's presence in the unit and to stay downstairs.

"Gary, he's up here all the time just laughing and yukking it up. He's so loud my headphones don't even drown him out. I can't concentrate when I have to keep looking over my shoulder to make sure he doesn't come after me again."

"Oh, I'm sure he won't do that. He's going to be careful, especially now"—meaning, now that he's in trouble again.

About a year after the blowup in the computer room, I was in the model shop with Kirk getting things ready for our next trip to the Body Farm. I was on the phone with the contract officer when Brent walked in and sat at his bench, ostensibly to work. After a minute or so, I noticed him drumming his fingers loudly and huffing and puffing dramatically. I looked to Kirk, with a "what's his problem?" expression.

Kirk rolled his eyes and said, "Nothing, just ignore him."

The thought passed through my mind that he was irritated at my being there, but I didn't want to be paranoid. I ignored him, finished the call, and left.

It turns out, I wasn't being paranoid. The next day, an "all-hands" email came down from on high, reminding us that we shouldn't be making lengthy personal calls on a coworker's phone. Management hates nothing more than dealing with issues directly, so the email was addressed to everyone in the unit. I would have bet a paycheck that Brent had gone to his supervisor complaining about me, and I knew the drill. If I didn't set the record straight, I'd get dinged on my yearly evaluation for not "working well with others."

I wrote back to the supervisor explaining that I had made a call using the unit phone on the wall, not at a coworker's desk, it was all work-related, and I kept the call as short as possible. I copied Brent and Kirk on the email, since they were the others who were present.

Within minutes, Brent emailed me: "STOP LYING. Or do we need a meeting?" This didn't sound like a request for a calm conversation among adults. More like he wanted to beat me up at recess. But it was Friday, and I was going to be out of town for a weeklong course on forensic anthropology. I had already planned to go home early because it was a beautiful afternoon, and I was looking forward to a week filled with skulls and lectures on forensics. I didn't want my good mood ruined.

Apparently, my lack of a response infuriated Brent even more, because about fifteen minutes later he flung open the door to the Graphic Unit and stormed over to my cubicle.

"Where's Bailey?!" he thundered to no one in particular.

When told that I had left for the day, he snorted, "Oh, snuck her little ass out early, huh?" Brent prided himself on using his bulk to intimidate people, but his bubble soon burst.

"Actually, no. She had already scheduled leave for the rest of the day."

All this drama was unfolding as I was driving home, so when my phone rang, I had no idea what to expect. I answered, and a deep voice bellowed, "You've got a problem!" *Click.*

What the heck . . . ? Without my glasses, I couldn't see the number that had called, so I hit redial, and Brent answered. Eeeek! I instantly hung up.

I had forgotten about him the second I walked out of the door, but now he had gotten me good and mad. Getting harassed and threatened at work was one thing, but having it bubble over into my personal time was another. I was *not* putting up with this bullshit, and I wasn't going to let a week go by without making management deal with it, or it would just get brushed under the rug again.

I did a 180 and made the forty-five-minute drive back to work, going straight to Gary's office, who knew instantly why I was there. He shrugged and said, "I don't know what I can do about it. Ron is out. You can always go to Mr. Bean." He was the section chief, next in the chain of command, and the one who had given the verbal reprimand to Brent the year before. I'm sure Gary knew this was going to escalate, because he knew me. I wasn't going to let it go. Either upper management was going to do something about Brent, or I would.

Mr. Bean's door was open, so I looked in and saw he and the human resources unit chief, FELICIA GRUEL, were talking.

"It's OK, Lisa, come on in, we were done with our meeting."

Felicia got up to leave, but I said, "This might be something you want to stay for." This was a human resources issue if there ever was one. I didn't want to be dramatic, but I had to say my piece as quickly and calmly as I could. I took a deep breath and said, "Several times in the past two years I have been verbally and physically threatened by a coworker, and I need it to stop."

That got their attention.

"Tell me what's going on. Who is this coworker?" Mr. Bean asked.

He didn't seem too surprised at hearing Brent's name. I got a few words out. Then Brent's supervisor was called in along with security, and I recounted everything. Thankfully, they looked shocked and concerned. I was so used to being blown off when I raised an issue about something that seemed to be important, like my physical safety.

After I got back from the anthropology course I was called in by MR. FRANCO, the man above Mr. Bean. Yikes. I didn't know if I was in trouble or not; I hadn't been in the office for a week. Normally, when you go into an executive manager's office, they are sitting behind a big oak desk, and you take your spot across from them in a wobbly chair. Not this time. Mr. Franco stood up and welcomed me into his office, shook my hand, and sat down beside me.

I respected Mr. Franco and figured this was a page from Management 101 as a way to present a friendly demeanor while using body language to telegraph, *Please don't sue us, please don't sue us.*

"Tell me everything."

I finished talking, and I could see the muscles in his jaw work. This was not a guy to be trifled with. He assured me that things would be taken care of, and from now on Brent would know better than to try to intimidate me or anyone else in the unit.

I wouldn't want to say *I told you so* to upper management, but whatever consequences Brent faced weren't enough to prevent future outbursts.

Other than the ongoing incursions with Brent, I was thrilled with the reorganization. Crime-scene surveying and demonstrative evidence would stay in the Graphic Unit, and all the design and facial imaging work would go to the Photo Unit. The number of skulls coming into the lab would be growing exponentially too. Instead of one or two cases a year, Wade and I were asked if we could complete ten to fifteen each. *Would that be OK?* they asked. Are you kidding? We were thrilled!

I had been working hard to carve a spot out for myself as a subject matter expert in facial approximation before Wade was hired. He was very well-known in the community and had twenty years of experience under his belt as a composite artist and facial approximation expert. But if anyone expected a rivalry between us, they were sorely disappointed. We became teammates, not competitors. Now, there was somebody else who was as geeked out as I was about skulls and facial approximation. I could run over to his cube and say, "Oh my God, Wade, you've got to see the styloid process on this guy!" and he'd tell me whenever a new skull came in with something we had never seen before, like three extra teeth, or cranial sutures that should have been fused but weren't.

Everyone got along even better than we had down in the Graphic Unit, since now we were all together in one space and had time to get to know each other better. We worked just as hard as ever, but now we could joke around a bit during the day, talk about the news or Hollywood gossip, and go out to lunch together over at the academy cafeteria. I was feeling that same camaraderie that I had at Hopkins.

A supervisor who runs a group of senior artists with excellent work records truly has an easy time of it. Just hand us a job and it'll get done. That's what Gary had done, and when he left we had no expectations that anything would change. Usually first-line supervisor positions are filled from within the ranks, so that meant anyone who got the job would be one of our coworkers.

We were all a bit surprised when HARRY DUNNE was chosen for the job, but we were more than OK with it. He had known us all for years; we had worked on cases together and traveled together, so he knew what the job was about and knew our capabilities.

Harry and I had gone to several crime scenes before and always worked well together. One case especially sticks out in my mind; a woman had been sexually assaulted by a man who had broken into her house and waited for her for God knows how long. The part that gave me chills was that you could imagine where the confrontation was.

She had a rifle for protection and must have heard a noise eventually; there were bullet holes in the top of the door coming from the bedroom into the hall. I instantly pictured the intruder grabbing the end of the rifle. It goes off, and of course he takes it away from her. Now, she's helpless. From the looks of the photos, she fought like hell, but he had her trapped in her own home.

We were at lunch talking to the case agent when he said, "A security alarm might have saved her life." It was all so incredibly sad, and horrifying. She had no reason to think that she needed a security alarm. She lived in a nice area, knew her neighbors, and they all watched out for each other. The crime rate in that area was almost nonexistent, and violent crime was rare. Even leaving doors unlocked wasn't unusual.

But you just never know who's out there. In this case, it was a man who was out on parole, staying at his brother's house down the road from her. He had a long record of sexual assault, including attempted murder, and it wasn't a week after leaving prison before he claimed his next victim. He raped her, slashed her throat, and then defecated on the floor next to her body.

The whole experience really shook me. Harry and I were staying in a small motel, which I didn't like because it opened to the outside. I was a bit jittery and unsettled after diagramming the cabin and knowing what had happened there, so even though I told myself I was being ridiculous, I shoved an armchair under the doorknob. I wasn't going to tell anyone back at work, because I would probably get teased for being nervous, and wasn't about to tell Harry either. But the next morning at the Waffle House, he told me he had done the exact same thing.

Randall was the only fly in the ointment. When he reappeared from whatever sojourn he had been on, he was transferred to the

Photo Unit along with us. He was less happy about it than we were, and after a few months he was able to talk his way back down into the Graphic Unit. None of us put up a fight over that.

For years, people had whispered about how he must have had friends in high places because he was like Teflon. No wrongdoing ever stuck to him. When a colleague and I saw him greet a senior executive from the front office with squeals of delight, kisses on the cheek and a great big bear hug, we were amused. When we were called on the carpet and sternly told to "forget what we had seen," we were frightened. *Mum's the word.* I wish I had never witnessed it in the first place.

––––––––––––––

A few years before the reorganization, Gary called me into his office to talk about the facial imaging class. I was the team leader, which is a fancy way of saying I was responsible for putting together the syllabus and instruction manuals, reserving the classrooms, collaborating with the Training Unit, vetting student applications, and a thousand other things that must be put in place to get fourteen students from various parts of the world into one classroom for three weeks of instruction.

"We're going to reorganize the class," Gary said. "Facial approximation and postmortem imaging are coming out. We need to use that time to focus on composites and add more hands-on time for cognitive interviewing and courtroom testimony. Plus, I want to use all FBI employees from now on. I've already talked to someone who teaches at the academy, and she'd be perfect. Can you coordinate with her schedule and find other instructors for the next class?"

That was only a few months away, but I said yes without hesitation. We had talked about this topic many times over the past year, and I could tell Gary's mind was made up.

Facial approximation was always a very interesting section of the course, but as years passed, we could see that the training was doing

more harm than good. It's a twist of "a little learning being a dangerous thing," because it takes a whole lot longer than a week to become
proficient at something as complex as facial approximation.

The students were getting frustrated too: they had been introduced
to a fascinating subject but knew they might never have the opportunity to use it in the field. Most of the class attendees were dual-duty
artists working in state and local agencies and spent the majority of
their time on composite sketches. Every forensic artist wants to get
their hands on a skull one day, but it could be years before it happened, if ever.

Cost was another factor. Paying for guest instructors was expensive
and getting more costly each year as they raised their rates. Maybe
the FBI has a lot of money, but by the time it trickles down to the
individual units it's like street dogs fighting for scraps.

The revamped facial imaging class was a rousing success. The class
had gone back to its roots, preparing artists for the work they would be
doing the most, and adding more time on cognitive interviewing and
courtroom testimony. The front office was happy at the cost savings,
and we were able to harness the expertise of other FBI employees at
the academy.

A psychologist from the FBI's behavioral science unit came in to
teach cognitive interviewing. Yes, that's the same unit that was featured in *Silence of the Lambs*. And yes, it's in a basement three levels
below the cafeteria. The first thing that greets you as you walk in the
door is a mannequin of Anthony Hopkins in an orange jumpsuit and
leather mask sitting inside a cage. He's either holding a can of fava
beans—or maybe it was sitting on the floor, I forget. But either way
it was hilarious. One of the agents told us that it had been a gift from
a group of students at the academy.

The full arsenal of the bureau was brought in to teach. Even role
players from the FBI agent training program were tapped for interviewing practice. If the students came on too brusquely in their composite

sketch interview, the role players would react like real victims; they would turn away, shut down, and maybe even cry. If the students self-corrected, the actors responded in kind and would compose themselves to finish the description.

I was able to snag the same interview rooms that the agents used, and students would do the sketch while being videotaped. Then they'd get to watch their interview and critique themselves while talking to the psychologist about what they did right and how they could improve. We even did a mock court, with real FBI lawyers grilling the students on the stand while they testified to the composite they had done with the role player.

Wade took the lead on teaching composite sketching since he had more than twenty years of experience at it. TED and I would act as witnesses for the students to interview, and also help them with any shading or drawing issues.

When I wasn't in the class, you'd see me running between the academy and the lab putting out the fires that inevitably pop up. Usually, that's a metaphor, but one day we all arrived at the academy to find out there had been an actual fire in the building, so using our assigned classroom was out. Wade, Ted, and I spent a frenzied hour with carts moving all the students' materials to a new room, and they got there just as we were finishing the transition.

I was doubly excited about the future of the Body Farm. When we started, there were fifty skulls to collect, but as time went on more donor skulls became available. I had bumped into one of the directors at a forensic anthropology conference who told me they were asking for, and getting, more photos than ever before. They now had pictures of people from elementary school, high school, college, weddings, and even fiftieth anniversaries. Not only could we study facial approximation, but we could also use the collection for studying age progression.

With plenty of training material from the Body Farm collection we would be able to have a facial approximation class at the FBI Academy.

Wade and I could teach it, and just like the composite class, it would be offered free of charge to law enforcement employees.

It would be revolutionary. Before (in the old FBI class) there had only been enough time for the students to learn the very basics of the technique by sculpting on one generic skull with no life photo to analyze. With a three-week class solely on facial approximation and postmortem imaging, students might be able to work on six or eight skulls, if not more. Then there would still be the rest of the collection that they were free to study.

Momentum was building on all sides. When I found out that a team from a university in Scotland came to scan the collection about a year after our first trip, I beamed. When I first suggested the project, there had been a lot of quizzical looks, both inside and outside the FBI. People had trouble envisioning its significance. Maybe they felt: *If it was such a great idea, why hadn't it occurred to anyone before?* But now that an academic institution was following suit, I felt validated.

I'm not a pessimist, but when things are going extraordinarily well, I can get a bit antsy. *Is there something going on that I don't know about? What's coming around the bend? Is there an anvil about to drop out of the sky and take me out?* We were six months into the reorganization, and life in the Photo Unit couldn't have been any better.

I had the best job in the world, terrific coworkers, and a cherry on top: windows! In my entire working life, I had never once had a window in my office. I was always stuck in dank basements or in dark rooms protected by cipher locks inside windowless buildings wrapped in barbed wire. Now, I could look up from my desk with a sigh of contentment and watch the deer munching on the lawn in front of the laboratory while helicopters filled with marines in tactical gear flew overhead. I was in heaven.

8

Pit of Despair

When I worked at the National Security Agency during my time in the navy, management drilled it into our heads that we could never, ever tell anyone where we worked. "If someone asks, just say you work for the government." Of course, any time you answered that, the person got a knowing look on their face and said, "So you must work at the NSA!"

It was easier to say "I work in a candy store" than go through the farce of pretending I didn't work at the nation's number-one super-secret spy agency. I really had worked in a Russell Stover candy store when I was a teenager, so I could sound knowledgeable if anyone got into the finer points of the work. I knew all the chocolate swirls by heart and could spot the difference between a roman nougat or peanut chew with ease.

The guidance for these types of situations wasn't much better at the FBI. In fact, it was nonexistent. We could identify ourselves as FBI employees online but couldn't "give it any undue prominence," whatever that means. It wasn't until 2012, a full eight years after Facebook launched, that the FBI came out with a very vague, very unhelpful set of guidelines on social media. There was nothing specific, no hard regulations to follow, nothing to hang your hat on to protect yourself. It was just "choose a strong password" and "check your user settings." As of this writing, you can still find it on the FBI website because it still hasn't been updated.

With the lack of any specific guidance, almost everyone, myself included, decided to just follow common sense. I never identified myself as an FBI employee online. If there was a hot topic in the news that involved the FBI, I kept my opinion to myself. The same goes for politics and religion, so I never posted anything more controversial than a video of my cat Ace with his head stuck in a bag of potato chips.

But there's no way to put the toothpaste back in the tube when the agency itself is the one who is putting your name out there. I had never identified or promoted myself as an FBI employee, but the bureau sure had. I had been interviewed by NPR and the *Washington Post*, several online news outlets, and was even in a video on the FBI's YouTube channel.

All this unwanted attention made it too easy for people on the outside to contact me. It's not that hard to guess a person's work email address when you're in the federal government. It's inevitably some variation of the person's name (lisabailey? lbailey? lgbailey?), followed by the @ symbol, the agency acronym (three guesses!), and then ".gov." So all a person has to do is send a barrage of emails with all different versions of a person's name, and sooner or later they'll hit paydirt. This is the whole reason the FBI advises us not to say where we work on social media, and I hadn't done it—they had.

In the years since the TV show *CSI* debuted in 2001, interest in forensic jobs skyrocketed. Anyone and everyone who wanted to become a forensic artist now had somebody to ask. These were complete strangers, calling and emailing me at work, asking if I would look at their drawings, or help them get a job at the FBI, or write to them and give them advice. Reid put it best: "It's like calling a hospital and asking how to become a doctor."

There were rambling emails from people who thought the FBI was spying on them, angry and conspiratorial emails, and others so disturbing I reported them to security.

One email especially hit me in between the eyes, but it wasn't sent to me. A retired forensic artist sent a bitter letter of complaint to a senior executive in FBI management. She had come across my website about forensic art—and didn't approve. According to her, the site lacked "professional decorum" and was an embarrassment to the field of forensic art. Her email carried significant weight, because she had been a guest instructor at the FBI Academy and was a prominent member of several forensic art organizations.

I was dumbstruck. And hurt. This was someone I had known for years, a woman I had respected, admired, and looked up to. It was bad enough feeling like a chump because I thought we were friends. But much worse than that, I was now in FRANK HART's crosshairs. Her letter had worked its way down from the top of the management chain, landed on his desk, and I was called on the carpet to answer to her accusations.

This was my first major interaction with Frank, my new Unit Chief, and it wasn't pleasant. Just a whisper of unprofessionalism is enough to subject a person to disciplinary action in the FBI. I had wanted to stay under the radar, especially because I was new to the Photo Unit. But with that letter, I had a spotlight on me. And things started going south.

One day I was in the studio preparing a skull to be photographed. Harry walked past me, abruptly stopped, and doubled back. He stood in between me and the photographer and demanded, "What are you doing?"

It seemed sort of obvious since I was in the studio and had a skull sitting on a tripod with a camera in front of it, but I answered, "Just getting this skull photographed."

"Huh. So, you just set this all up by yourself?"

There was a hard tone in his voice that took me by surprise. At first, I thought he was joking, like the guy who walks up to a person milking a cow and says, "What are you doing?" It was just so odd for him to question me on something that was an innocuous, routine part of my job.

"Well, yes. It's a 2D approximation. It's part of the process." Harry should have understood this, what with being a forensic artist and all, but it didn't seem to be enough for him.

"So, calling the photographers, getting a work request, you never thought to come to me first?"

Why would I? Now, I was utterly confused, and you could almost see the question mark hovering over the photographer's head too. What was Harry's deal? This was like raising your hand to go to the bathroom; I was a senior artist doing my job.

"I'm sorry, Harry. I don't understand what's wrong. This is standard procedure; it's how it's always been done."

"You don't understand? Maybe you just don't *want* to understand."

I could feel my face get flushed and hot. I felt like a kid being chastised—in front of my coworkers, no less. What was with his attitude? This was not the Harry that we knew in the Graphic Unit. This was Harry with some kind of agenda.

"So . . . do you want me to come to you before I put in a work request to have a skull photographed?" I ventured.

"No, I just need to know what's going on. I'm your supervisor."

My inner monologue snarked, *You should already know what's going on, because you're the one who assigned me this case.* But of course, I couldn't vent that out loud. So I just stood there, waiting for him to get done with whatever was going on in his brain.

Finally satisfied that he had chastised me long enough for no reason, he left. This was probably the fifth 2D facial approximation that the photographer and I had worked on together, and nothing like this had ever happened before. He could see that I was rattled, and he patted me on the shoulder sympathetically.

What the heck had just happened?

A sheriff's office called Harry because they had been getting repeated calls from a young woman whose mother had been missing for years and was insisting that an age progression be done. Harry accepted the job, which he absolutely should *not* have done.

Stay with me; I'm not a heartless person.

With age progressions and approximations, the supervisor gathers enough information during the initial call with the agent or detective and makes a determination. It saves everyone a lot of time and frustration to let them know that while the FBI artists are good, we are not miracle workers. We also can't do every case that comes down the pike. There are just some situations where forensic art isn't going to bring anything new or helpful to a case.

In this instance, a woman had gone to prison when her daughter was ten years old but didn't return home after she was released. She had been picked up by her sister at the prison gate but then insisted on being dropped off at a motel, the same motel where she had been initially arrested. When she didn't return after a few days, the sister filed a missing person report. Ten years later she was still gone.

By then, the daughter was twenty years old and insistent that something had happened to her mother to prevent her from returning. She wanted an age progression done and for the police to help find her mother. But how? They had gone to the motel after she had been reported missing, but the leads went nowhere.

It would be different if the mother had been a fugitive, but she wasn't. She had served her time and was free to go where she wanted. And if she didn't want to go home, that was her business. Maybe "home" was where her abusive husband lived. Maybe home was where her problems stemmed, and she wanted to start fresh elsewhere. Maybe she thought her daughter was better off without her, maybe there were mental health issues, maybe there were a thousand other reasons why she didn't return home. Adults are allowed to walk away from their life, and no amount of law enforcement intervention can force them to return.

While the case of the missing mother was sad, it does not constitute a matter for the FBI to be involved in. Or even the police. An age progression could be done, but then what? The sheriff's office didn't have the manpower to investigate a ten-year missing persons case, especially when there was nothing to indicate the woman had been in danger. It all comes full circle: adults are allowed to go missing.

I did the best I could with the only image of the mother available: her arrest photo. If this had been a fugitive case, I would have gone on the more plausible scenario that she was living under the radar with little to no money, and age her appropriately. I didn't see any point in that and decided to do a kinder, more optimistic version. A little extra weight to fill out her cheeks, a nice hairdo, just a touch of makeup and a slight smile. I figured it couldn't do any harm, so why not do a best-case scenario? After all, it might be the only image the girl would ever have of her mom.

It was summer vacation, and I was sixteen. I loved old movies, and was watching *Bathing Beauty* from 1944, with Esther Williams and Red Skelton. It's one of those ridiculous but wonderful movies from the Hollywood studio days where Esther swims in full makeup and

Skelton somehow inexplicably winds up in a pink tutu in ballet class. Skelton was my brother Steve's favorite comedian, and I remember thinking how he would have especially loved this part, because he had danced in the ballet before joining the marines.

During the '70s, being a male dancer, especially when you're in high school, "was for sissies." But nobody could bully Steve. Jokes at his expense fell flat because he didn't give a hoot what anybody said or thought. He sailed through boot camp, laughing at the notoriously rigorous training. "Three months at Parris Island was a piece of cake. Try getting your ass kicked all day in a ballet class!"

There was a knock at the door. I opened it and saw two marines and a military chaplain. I didn't process what this meant immediately. It was more like, *We're not Catholic, why is a priest here?*

"Are your parents home?" one of them asked.

Steve had actually written a few months before saying, "Boy, you guys came really close to collecting $20,000 today. I nearly fell off a cliff hiking!" Always the adventurer, nothing ever scared Steve, not even a brush with death. He went right on hiking cliffs in Hawaii, and died when the rain-soaked ground fell away beneath him.

There was no open casket viewing because of Steve's injuries. The last time I saw him was when he was home on leave, laughing, spit-shining his shoes to a mirror finish, and eating peanut M&M's while saving all the red ones for last. And that's the way I want to remember him.

After I became a forensic artist, I was often asked, "Why don't you do an age progression of him?"

"Why in the world would I do that?" I replied. I didn't mean to be harsh, but the thought repulsed me, and still does. I don't need Photoshop to picture my brother, not at nineteen, and not even as he might be today, in his sixties.

There's a cottage industry of artists who do age progressions of the deceased, but it's not for me. And I've been asked more times than I can count.

"I lost my baby when he was nine months old . . ."

"My daughter died when she was twelve, can you do a picture of her in a wedding dress?"

"My husband and I are infertile, can you do a picture of what a child of ours might have looked like?"

The stories are heartbreaking, but I can't bring myself to do them.

I had done one in the past, and even though it didn't involve death, I will never do it again. I was asked if I could do age progressions of two little girls, sisters. They were alive and well, but their father was going blind and wanted to see what they might look like when they were adults. I didn't know the people, but it was a friend of a friend, and I felt obligated, even though I shouldn't have. I would do it on my own time after work, and wouldn't charge anything, but the only thing was, they would need to be done as quickly as possible because of the father's degenerating eyesight.

Worse than realizing that I should have been strong enough to decline was what happened after I said yes. My mom had a stroke, which resulted in weeks of being out of the office, sleeping in hospital chairs, cleaning out my mom's apartment, arranging for her to go to assisted living, selling her condo and car. . . . It was a nightmare. It was awful, and beyond exhausting.

Besides being worried sick about my mom, I also had the pressure of getting the photos done before the man went completely blind. I wouldn't let myself renege; they didn't have time to find another artist. And if they did, it would cost a lot of money. Besides, I had promised.

I got them done in time, and the wife sent me a beautiful letter thanking me, but it tore me apart. I had come to believe that it wasn't my place to plant those images in another person's head. I was only an artist, and I didn't have that right. I hope he forgot what those photos looked like, because he should be able to picture his own versions of his daughters, not something that I did in Photoshop.

Just as the case of the missing mother shouldn't have come to the FBI, the next one shouldn't have, either. Harry got a call involving a standoff situation, where a man had barricaded himself in his house. He was threatening to kill himself, his family, and anyone else who came near. The man would not identify himself, but authorities on the scene believed they knew who it was, a murder suspect who had been wanted for several years.

My email dinged. It was Harry instructing me to prepare an age progression of the suspect's last arrest photo so officers could compare it to the man in the house. Oh, and by the way, you need to have it done within an hour. I read the email from Harry twice to make sure I wasn't hallucinating before I went to his office.

"Harry, is this right? They want an age progression as a way to positively ID this guy?"

"Yes, what's the problem?"

"It's impossible, and it's dangerous! I could do an age progression and it might look like the guy in the house, but that doesn't mean it's him. Whoever requested this has been watching too much TV or just doesn't understand how this works."

"Look, I already promised it to him, so just do it."

I called the officer and made it abundantly clear that any image I came up with was NOT to be used for identification purposes. Thankfully nothing came of it; the man gave himself up without getting shot.

But still . . . this kind of stuff was dangerous, and happening more and more often. I would be working on a job that Harry had assigned me, and then I'd walk past Wade's desk and notice that he was working on the same thing. I'd be scrambling to get a last-minute presentation done, only to find out that the client had submitted it weeks before.

One time, he had actually accepted an age progression of a man who had been declared legally dead. There was plenty of other work on my plate, and I knew it would be a colossal waste of time and effort to chase after a corpse.

Logic finally won out, and the assignment was canceled. I did some digging on my own after work and found out the request had come from a group of retired detectives who started an informal cold case group on Facebook and wanted to post the age progression for leads. Or likes.

Wade, Ted, and I started comparing notes and tallied how often these sorts of things were happening. That's when we came to the only natural conclusion: Harry was wholly unprepared for a position in management.

He was supremely disorganized, and you could tell him the same thing over and over, but he wouldn't remember. If he didn't know something, he'd make it up, and when he made mistakes (which was happening more and more often), he would blame us. More than once, we heard him inside Frank's office saying, "They're messing things up on purpose to make me look bad." What was worse is that Frank accepted it without question.

We knew Frank wasn't exactly thrilled to have us in his unit. In our very first group meeting he said, "I don't know why you're here, or what you do, but it looks like I'm stuck with you." As time went on, "less than thrilled" turned into essentially "hated our guts." We didn't understand why and weren't prepared for the venom that came our way. In the Graphic Unit we were professionals; in the Photo Unit we were treated like unruly toddlers.

Frank liked to rule with an iron fist, even though all the employees who reported to him were professionals and didn't need to be micromanaged or cowed into working. The lack of women in senior professional roles couldn't be ignored either. All the senior photographers in the "studio," the ones who documented evidence and deployed to crime scenes, were men. Whenever a female photographer tried to advance into the studio, she was told she "might be ready in a few years." And according to Frank, no woman was ever ready for the studio.

Here's how forensic art gets done in the FBI, or at least how it's supposed to: When an FBI field agent needs graphic assistance, she writes a synopsis of the case and sends a message via the FBI case database. That request is called a "lead." In the movies it would sound like, "Hey chief, we got a lead on the murder suspect, we need to get on this pronto." But in the FBI, a lead is simply a request from an agent in a field office for the recipient to do something. Each lead has a case number, so anyone working that case can check on its progress at any time in the database.

All unit chiefs and supervisors in case-working units are supposed to be logged into the database continuously, and the computer would ding when a new lead came in. If the person wasn't at their desk to hear the ding, he would see an alert symbol when he logged back on. If he *still* missed it, there would be another alert in another window of the database. When an agent wants you to do something, it's pretty hard to ignore.

When that lead comes in, it's purpose is to notify the unit chief of the cases that are coming into the unit, and to prompt the supervisor to act on—meaning, assign—the case to one of the artists. Somehow Harry managed to ignore leads from agents all the time, and in this particular case it was a request for an age progression of a fugitive wanted on federal charges. It was a routine ten-year update of a suspect, so it didn't have an urgent deadline, but still, just get the darn thing done. But Harry wouldn't respond to the lead. Over the course of six months, the agent had been calling and emailing Harry, leaving voicemails, and pinging him in the database.

Finally, the status of the case escalated, and I could imagine the agent gritting his teeth as he wrote to Harry one more time: "We are scheduled to shoot a news program that will air across the entire Western Hemisphere during the second week of July. Any assistance you could lend in getting us something to include in the program would be greatly appreciated." This was the very last resort for the agent, short of flying to Quantico and standing on Harry's desk. Still, crickets chirped.

I didn't know any of this had been going on until the agent stepped out of protocol and emailed me, asking, "Is there any way you can get Harry to respond to my lead without getting yourself in hot water?" I had done age progression work for this agent before, true. But it's standard procedure to contact the supervisor first, and he knew it could blow back on me.

I called the agent back and told him the only thing I could. "Call Frank." Yes, I was worried he would see this as insubordination—*How dare you imply that Harry is dropping the ball?* But it had to be done. Not five minutes later, I got an email from Harry, oblivious to his neglect of the case and shifting blame to the agent. "He kept emailing me, but this is an age progression you've already done."

No, Harry, it's not. I knew pointing out his mistake wouldn't do any good. The agent knew which end was up, and that's all that really mattered.

―――――――――――

The FBI doesn't just work on federal cases, it is also there to assist with local law enforcement at no charge. All the FBI asks for is a written request on agency letterhead to get the ball rolling. With that, an FBI case number is assigned with a special acronym that defines it as local assistance (rather than federal), and that letter is the first thing that goes in the case file.

This system makes sure that any case the FBI is involved with is logged, and helps to potentially connect dots between cases. For instance, in the Graphic Unit we might get a request to do a composite sketch for a sexual assault that happened in Virginia. But for all anyone knows, it might turn out that the assailant is a serial rapist, and there are similar cases in other parts of the United States. That case number, starting with the request letter, is what gets the composite "in the system," where agents might be able to compare it with other cases throughout the country.

We still assisted with local cases when we went to the Photo Unit, but after a while I noticed that there wasn't any case number on the assignments in the database. Maybe Harry had forgotten to type them in, so I went to his office to ask.

"What do you mean, a case number? This is for a sheriff's office."

"I know. But there was always a case number when we did them in the Graphic Unit."

Harry snorted and said, "No, all we need is a request from the sheriff's office on their letterhead, and I got that."

"But . . . then that's what's used to get the case number, right?"

Harry ignored my question, gave me an exaggerated sigh, and said, "Look, I've got all the letters right here." He opened his desk drawer and pulled out a manila folder with a stack of copies as proof. "Satisfied?"

No, actually. Letters sitting in a folder meant that none of the composite cases we had worked on had any way of being tracked. I tried to explain that to him, but I wasn't getting anywhere and had to let it go, at least for the time being.

One day Harry called me into his office and said, "You need to turn in your BlackBerry." Gary had issued one to me a few years before, meaning that I was now entrusted with traveling to do composites or deploy to crime scenes. At the time, a BlackBerry was an essential item for case-working employees.

I had to ask: "Why?"

"Because I said so."

Because you said so? There had to be a valid reason.

"Harry, really, why? Am I getting a replacement?"

"No. I'm telling you to turn it in because you don't need it."

"But I do, that's why Gary assigned it to me."

Harry sighed heavily and said, "Just use your own cell phone."

"But I pay for my phone out of pocket, and I'm not supposed to use it for bureau business. That's what the BlackBerries are for."

Of course, BlackBerries are never used for classified information, but they were a much more reliable form of communication when on travel, at least back in 2009. My cell phone didn't even work inside the building, but the BlackBerry would.

"I've already said no. Your phone is good enough."

"Do Ted and Wade have to turn in their BlackBerries too?"

"That's none of your business." Harry snapped.

Well, I knew what that meant. Of course not.

The other consequence of my not having a BlackBerry was that I had to list my personal cell phone number in the FBI directory. I wasn't an on-call employee, and I didn't appreciate my number being out there for everyone to see. Not that anyone would do something nefarious; it was just the principle of the thing. Why did Wade and Ted get to keep their BlackBerries, but not me?

Then Harry came after my laptop, announcing that it would be reassigned to Ted.

"But I need my laptop when I travel for composites, that's why Gary issued it to me."

"I told you it's being transferred to Ted. End of discussion."

Ted was as flummoxed as I was. He rarely went on travel, so now this was just one more inventory item he'd have to keep track of. But I used it all the time. We didn't have Internet stations at our desk, and I used it to contact students for the facial imaging class. I also used it for emailing composite sketches while on travel, editing photographs, and all the other wonderful things that laptops allowed me to do.

I couldn't use my own laptop, because that's against security rules and I'd be written up. Now, every time I was called out on travel (often with only several hours' notice) I had to scramble to borrow a laptop and jump through all the security hoops to change permission settings and passwords. More than once, I'd be out on a job and realize that I couldn't save a file or make changes because I didn't have the authority.

But Harry wouldn't budge, so I signed over my laptop to Ted, where it sat in a drawer until he retired.

Then there was the matter of the 3D software for processing skull scans. Until now, we had piggybacked on the software licenses from the Graphic Unit and I needed a copy. But Harry and Frank wouldn't get it for me. All that needed to be purchased was something called a "dongle." It's a little thing that looks like a USB drive, that would allow me to access the software. They had issued the software license to Wade, but again, they simply refused to get me my own copy. When I asked how I was supposed to get my skulls processed, they told me, "Wade can do it."

Wade could see exactly what was going on, so he fit my skulls in with his without complaint, even though it took time away from his own cases. It also made it harder for me to meet my deadlines, because I had to wait for him to process his jobs as well as mine. My facial approximation cases would sit gathering dust whenever he was out of town, either for official duty travel or on vacation. Perversely, it also allowed Harry and Frank to mark me down on my yearly evaluation because I wasn't processing my own work.

If I had been wearing a uniform with epaulets, he probably would've ripped those off too. I had spent ten years at the FBI working my way up the ladder, proving that I had the chops to do all the work. I was an accomplished forensic artist, and now I was being kicked back down, relegated to second-class citizen status. And there wasn't a darn thing I could do about it.

Even though the situation wasn't funny in the least, it became a running joke between me and Wade, "You know, Lisa, if you only had a dongle, you wouldn't get treated this way." And I had to laugh.

———————————

One year into my fresh circle of hell, the joke going around the unit was, "If Harry is yelling, then you know Lisa is in his office."

I'm no wilting flower, but I don't like to be barked at, especially for no reason. Nobody does, I guess, but I thought I should point that out because it seemed to be a foreign concept at the FBI.

I hadn't been yelled at so much since boot camp. Harry would tower over me, waving his arms around and not making an ounce of sense. Did you know that the length of your arms, when held out to both sides, is equal to your height? Harry was at least six foot four, so just imagine a seventy-six-inch wingspan coming at you. It was humiliating, unnerving to the point of being frightening, and it was happening more and more often.

There were two other supervisors in the unit who could hear Harry and Frank yelling—the walls were paper thin—and I used to hope that they would intervene. At the FBI, it's always drilled into our heads that managers are held to a higher standard and are duty-bound to report infractions or harassment. But they never did. They were both nice guys, but that's one thing they dropped the ball on.

You might be wondering why I didn't slip an iPhone into my pocket set to record. That way I'd have proof to bring to Mr. Bean, since he didn't seem to believe me when I told him how bad things were. But I couldn't, because using any recording device in FBI space is prohibited. I also knew that it was enforced, due to an incident that occurred to one employee years before.

He had a bullying supervisor who constantly yelled and made threats too, and his reports to upper management did no good, either. They didn't believe the supervisor's behavior could be all that bad, and the employee couldn't seem to make them understand the severity of what he was going through. (This wasn't at the laboratory; it happened in an entirely different division, but I'm detecting a trend here.) Anyway, he recorded one of the episodes and took it back up to the chain of command saying, "Here's the proof of my supervisor yelling and making threats against me." Upper management finally took notice, an investigation was immediately launched, and the guilty party was fired. Go ahead, guess who it was.

The employee. It didn't matter that the recording gave ample evidence of his supervisor's threats and bullying. The employee was fired for being desperate enough to resort to a recording device to prove that his supervisor was being abusive.

What floored me was the pontificating by the FBI office that handed out the punishment: "All employees must act with the utmost integrity, blah blah blah, and clearly this employee had violated that tenet of the FBI's code."

So, what about the supervisor, the one who did all the yelling and threats? Last I heard, he had been promoted.

Besides Harry screeching at me all the time and being hobbled in my work by the lack of BlackBerry, laptop, and dongle, Frank would find various and sundry ways to embarrass me and demean me.

Within a few weeks of transferring into the unit, I was called into his office while he was in a meeting with several male supervisors. After he got an answer to his question, he waved his hand and said, "You can go now. Quick, hop like a bunny!"

My head snapped back involuntarily because I was so shocked and insulted. Women everywhere know that if I had said anything back, I'd be branded a bitch, so I had to let it roll over me. Let everyone know I was an easygoing person who wouldn't make a federal case out of what might have been an innocent quip or slip of the tongue. The second time it happened, I stood stone-faced and glared at Frank while he smirked, and the other men in the room chuckled.

The third time it happened, I looked Frank in the eye and said without a trace of humor, and air quotes added for emphasis: "I am not a 'bunny,' and I do not 'hop.'" I looked around at the other supervisors to let them know I meant business. Their smiles vanished and the atmosphere in the room got very tense, very fast. I could tell Frank was furious, but I knew I had made my point, and I left.

The FBI always tells us that going to EEO (the agency's equal employment opportunity office) is an option, but in reality, nobody ever said the word aloud. It was only whispered into a trusted coworker's ear in the hallway, lest a supervisor walk by. In the bureau, EEO is fightin' words.

Going to EEO was the last thing I wanted to do. I had heard too many stories that even though complaints were supposed to be resolved in a timely manner, they took years to complete. That meant the employee was stuck enduring the behavior that caused them to file a complaint in the first place. Retaliation wasn't supposed to happen, but c'mon, who were they kidding?

Rumors were swirling that the reorganization would be reversed, so I hoped the problem would take care of itself. I had to figure out a way to survive until then.

9

Dumb and Dumber

What does a burned body look like? Well, some parts of it look like barbecued ribs, others like fried chicken. You know when the skin cracks and gets all bubbly and crispy, just the way you like it? It's like that. I was finding this out firsthand while standing in the inner sanctum of the Smithsonian's National Museum of Natural History next to a charred corpse.

Whenever a facial approximation is done from a skull, it's inherently a cold case, because the body was found as skeletal remains. Typically, by the time a skull makes it to an artist's desk, at least a year has gone by, or more often a decade—which gave this case a rare twist: I'd be doing a facial approximation from a body that turned up only the week before.

The problem was finding an imaging facility that would accept scorched, decomposing remains. Hospitals balk at that sort of thing, and I imagine patients would as well. CT scanners are meant for the living, and that means most morgues aren't equipped with them. When a medical examiner needs to look inside a body before an autopsy, she will use X-rays instead.

The police had been trying for days, and asked if the FBI could help. We didn't have a CT scanner at the time either, but I remembered that the Smithsonian did, using it for scanning mummies and artifacts. If they didn't mind having a two-thousand-year-old body in their scanner, I figured they might not mind a fresh one. CHRIS, one of the FBI anthropologists, had a number of professional contacts within the Smithsonian, so after a few calls it was all set.

Wade and I were packing up for the trip into DC and excitedly talking about how cool it was going to be. I had been to the Smithsonian before for the "not-Osama" skull, and had seen back rooms that weren't open to the general public, but certainly neither of us had been present for anything like this. It was a one-of-a-kind experience and would open up possibilities for being able to take on more cases like this in the future.

As if on cue, Harry walked in.

"What are you doing?"

"We're getting stuff ready to go to the Smithsonian."

"Smithsonian? What for?"

"The CT scan. The burned body in the dumpster, remember?"

"How come nobody tells me anything about this?"

Wade and I looked at each other. Here we go again.

"Harry, you assigned me the job. You've been copied on all the emails that had been going back and forth making arrangements. Wade and I are driving, and Chris is going to meet us up there. It's all set."

"I don't have time to read all those emails. I didn't know anything about this!"

Well, you would have if you'd read your emails. I couldn't possibly say that out loud, but I knew Wade was thinking it too.

"Who else did you say was going?"

"Chris."

"Why didn't Chris call me?"

"I don't know," I said cautiously. "It'd be better to ask them, but probably because it's more efficient to email and copy everyone rather than make lots of separate phone calls."

"Don't you see what the problem is? Nobody tells me anything, and I'm the supervisor!"

Harry was getting himself worked up, pacing, getting louder and louder and venting his anger at me.

"And why were you talking to Chris anyway?"

Completely flummoxed, I said, "Because I'm supposed to. Consulting with the anthropologist is part of our job."

"Well, I need to know about these things!"

I ventured, "How much do you want to know about? Are you saying you want me to ask you first before I talk to the anthropologist?"

"No! I only need you to tell me the important things."

This was a replay of his rant in the photo studio, but now in front of several more open-mouthed onlookers.

"Could you give me some guidelines? I mean, 'important' means different things to different people."

"I don't have time to write all that down! You're still not listening to me. Or maybe you just don't *want* to listen."

I give up. In less than twelve months as a supervisor, Harry had turned from a nice guy into a crazed, nonsensical bully. After he finally stomped out, Wade and I just looked at each other in disbelief. This shit was getting old.

CT scanners are huge, and this one was crammed into a small room with metal shelving on one side and a computer desk on the other. The attendants from the medical examiner's office started to push the gurney inside, but it wasn't about to fit without a lot of back-and-forth, like a really bad parallel parking job. Just as they got the gurney about halfway in the door, we all realized at the same time that I was still in the hallway, when I should have been inside already. After all their trouble, I couldn't ask them to move it back out, so I did the only thing I could. I tucked in my blouse, sucked in my breath, and did my darnedest to squeeze between the wall and the gurney without touching the gurney or the charred corpse.

Never in my wildest dreams did I imagine I'd ever be within millimeters of getting globs of human fat or pieces of burned flesh on my clothes. If I had on a lab coat, I would have been fine, but I knew I'd throw out anything as soon as I got home if I came in contact with anything "meaty."

I finally managed to get inside, and after a small smattering of jokey applause, motioned that it was OK to wheel her all the way in. All eyes were on me as I took photos, as they had nothing else to do. I concentrated on getting as many photos as I could in every conceivable angle. This was a rare opportunity to get more information about her face and features, and if she were ever identified it would be more information to add to the reference database.

Her hair was burned into a clump, and it was impossible to tell what the color had been, or whether it was straight or curly, but at least I could still tell where her hairline had been. The lips had been burned entirely away, and the side of her mouth had split wide open, displaying her upper and lower teeth, still in perfect condition.

The actual CT scan came next, and we were able to look at the skull on the computer right there at the lab. It was fascinating to see—none of us had ever expected to do anything like this. Combined with the photos, I'd have more information than ever before doing the approximation.

As it turned out, the woman was identified before I could finish, which made me happy. I would gladly give up doing facial approximations forever if it meant that victims were readily identified instead. But Harry and Frank didn't see it that way. To them, it had been a waste of time and money, giving them one more reason to come after me.

———————————

Finally, during one of Harry's more spectacular outbursts, I stood up and uttered a phrase that usually stops supervisors in their tracks: "I respectfully request an EEO counselor or neutral third party to be present." I had prepared that comment in advance according to the FBI's own regulations about bullying and hostile work environments. It's a not-so-subtle clue to a supervisor that they are out of line and one step away from an EEO complaint.

"No! Nobody needs to come in here."

"Yes, they do. I'm being yelled at for no reason, and I'm tired of it. I want someone else here as a witness."

"No!" he shouted. "You're being ridiculous! Sit down!"

Now, as many women have experienced, when a female speaks in a firm tone, voicing an opinion or statement of fact that is contrary to what a male has espoused, she is usually accused of being shrill and told to "calm down." You know, before she gets hysterical.

I kept right on standing. "No. Again, I respectfully request an EEO counselor or neutral third party to be present. You are making me extremely uncomfortable. Either someone comes in here, or I need to leave."

Why didn't I just walk out? Because that's insubordination. It's not really, of course, by definition. But that's how certain managers in the FBI operate, usually the ones who have never served in the military but like to boss people around like they're Patton. Still, with all the crap I'd been dealing with, I knew he'd try to take disciplinary action against me if I left.

It took one more round of yelling from him, and another declaration from me that I insisted on an EEO counselor's presence, for him to finally relent and blurt, "Fine, go ahead, go! Call GRACE!" referring to the EEO counselor for the laboratory.

I started back to my desk, but before I had a chance to pick up the phone, I was called into Frank's office.

The door hadn't closed behind me before Frank said abruptly, "Call off the lawyers. You don't get to contact EEO. That's my decision."

My stomach lurched. Oh my God! What world was I in? I know there are still plenty of supervisors everywhere who are deeply misogynistic and despise the fact that they are made to hide their true selves and play nice. But for him to come right out and say, "You don't get to call EEO"? I was in deep, deep trouble.

Frank declared that I had been the one to start the yelling, not Harry. "He had to yell at you to bring you back into control. You were out of line."

"But that's not what happened," I practically sputtered. "I never yelled at him."

"Yes, you did. Harry told me that's what happened. Are you calling him a liar?"

Now, I was really on shaky ground. Even hinting that a supervisor is lying is considered insubordination. "But I wasn't yelling," I insisted. "People outside the office heard what was happening. He was yelling at me, not the other way around."

Harry now weighed in, insisting that I was being hysterical (told you so), and he had never yelled at me . . . while he was yelling. As his voice rose higher and higher, I looked over at Frank in disbelief and said, "He's yelling at me right now."

Frank motioned to Harry with his hands, as though to say, *Bring it down.*

After a few moments I said, "I treat Harry respectfully, and all I ask is that he treat me the same." Going out on somewhat of a limb, I added, "He never talks this way to the men, it's only to me."

That subtle hint was ignored. I went on. "Look, I just don't want to be yelled at anymore. Everyone hears you yelling at me all the time, and they're making jokes about it. People stop me in the hallway. I've even been teased by people in other units."

Harry scoffed and said, "What do you care what people think?"

His response was unfathomable to me, and I said, "Because I work with them, and there's no reason to yell, ever."

All this went right over his head as Frank piped in, "I don't care what people say about me." No newsflash there. Frank was despised by half the people in the unit.

I went on. "I have to care about what people think, I have a professional reputation that I've worked really hard for, and it's damaging to my credibility if people think I'm some kind of troublemaker. I'm not, and I never have been."

Harry spoke again. "You know, Lisa, you seem to have trouble with a lot of people."

"What? Who? What do you mean?"

"I'm talking about Brent. You caused all that trouble with him."

I couldn't believe what I was hearing. Brent is the human tank who had backed me into a computer room two years before. Brent is the one who came after me again a year later, with more threats and a physical confrontation. Brent is the one who had confronted every single person in the unit at one time or another, but nobody had the nerve to point out that he was the common denominator or had the guts to report him.

Apparently, the definition of a troublemaker in the FBI is a person who refuses to be a punching bag, and forces management to do their job. Once the FBI finally leaped into action after his last tirade against me, Brent was suspended for ten days and appeared pacified when he slunk back to work. By now, it had been a whole year, and he hadn't threatened me since.

Still, this was all too much. "Harry, you know what happened! Brent has an anger problem. He came after me both those times! For Pete's sake, he's even gone after his own supervisor!"

I learned this gem only the day before, and it was the talk of the laboratory. Apparently, Brent's supervisor had the nerve to instruct Brent to attend a meeting, which resulted in Brent becoming indignant, which resulted in the supervisor becoming indignant, which resulted in both of them hurling insults until one of them, allegedly, chest-thumped the other. My money's on Brent.

"No," Harry said, shaking his head, "that's not it." A few moments passed until he started chuckling.

What now? I thought. *How can he possibly top that last one?*

Harry looked up and said, "I get it. It all makes sense. I know what the problem is." He pointed at me triumphantly and said, "You. You're the problem."

"What?! How can I be the problem?"

Harry kept pointing at me and laughing, marveling at his own genius. "Yep, that's it, all right. You're the problem. I can't believe I didn't see this before."

Frank agreed solemnly, "It's true. Your behavior does show a pattern. You need to watch yourself."

I could only stare at him in disbelief. If I didn't stop doing the absolute nothingness of what I was doing, other than existing in Brent's space-time continuum, then I was in big trouble.

Frank waved his hand and announced, "You're dismissed."

As I walked back to my desk, I could see my coworkers' eyes following me. I didn't cry. I wasn't about to, not there. Thank God it was Friday. I had already planned to take a half day off to spend time with my sister, Lauren. Somehow, I made the forty-five-minute drive home without an accident. I was so upset, I burst into tears the moment I saw her waiting for me in my driveway.

Reid was traveling, which meant we had the whole weekend to talk. Besides being sisters, Lauren and I are best friends. We can tell each other anything and are able to spend days on end doing nothing but hanging out and talking. We'll get into giggle fits over the stupidest thing, and never let more than a day go by without talking, texting, or sending each other ridiculous memes, like dogs riding bicycles or chickens wearing socks. She already knew everything that had been going on at work, and had been furious on my behalf, but it would be fair to say this latest episode made her incandescent with rage.

After a weekend of talking about work, watching movies, laughing, and (did I mention?) talking about work, Lauren convinced me to go talk to an EEO counselor.

That Monday I made an appointment with Grace, the counselor for the laboratory. At that time, EEO counselors were regular support staff who volunteered for the program. This was meant to make the process less intimidating, and I can attest that it absolutely did help. Counselors weren't part of management or human resources; they were one of us. I was more comfortable that what I said would remain confidential, and that trust was never broken.

We talked for over an hour. Everything I said in that meeting would be off the record, which is the way I wanted it. After I recounted everything that had been happening over the past year and a half, she urged me to consider mediation. I was still hesitant. I didn't want to make things worse than they already were.

Then Grace made a suggestion. She could go to Harry and Frank separately, voice my concerns, and then discuss options of how we could "move forward in a more productive way."

"Let's do that," I said. "Then they'll know I'm not trying to fire all torpedoes. I just want to be treated like a human being."

For most supervisors, that would be enough. Any supervisor with half a brain recognizes they have been given a gift. This is their opportunity to head off a formal EEO complaint, and it all stays off the record.

It didn't go well. "You won't believe what they said," Grace told me the next day. "They said that this was their way of managing you. And if you don't like it, you can quit."

———————————

What constitutes a "hit" in forensic art? It depends on who you ask. Because there's no recognized authority that oversees our profession, there's no agreed-upon definition, and that can lead to some questionable claims among forensic artists.

An undeniably perfect composite hit would look like this: an artist does a composite of a suspect in a home invasion. Police release the drawing, and a day later a member of the public thinks, *That looks like CARL*, so they call in a tip. Police do some digging, arrest Carl, compare his prints to the ones found all over the house, and sure enough, he's the guy. In forensic art circles nobody is going to make the argument that this wasn't a stone-cold hit.

But what if the drawing was released and nothing happened? And all leads came to dead ends? Five years later, Carl is picked up on burglary charges, literally caught in the act while rummaging through the liquor cabinet. His fingerprints are all over a different house with a different victim, and those get matched to the fingerprints in the original case from five years earlier.

Is that first drawing a hit? An artist can make that argument if he thinks it looks like Carl. After all, they did their job, and you can't account for bad luck and timing. If the drawing looks nothing whatsoever like Carl, the artist might still proclaim it a hit, because now the two cases are tied together, even though their drawing had nothing to do with it.

The whole subject gets very touchy and confrontational and enters into some muddy ethical waters. It's one thing to keep track of how your cases are resolved and use the experience to learn and get better. It veers into the area of commercialism and crassness when it becomes "How many cases can I take credit for solving?" After all, the artist wasn't the only person involved in bringing Carl to justice. What about the evidence technicians, fingerprint examiners, police officers, and (oh, by the way) the victim?

In facial approximation, hits are even trickier to define because, as you know, there are so many missing puzzle pieces, inefficient databases, and simple human error involved. For the sake of argument, a perfect facial approximation hit would go like this: a skull is found, a sculpture is done, and it's distributed online. A woman sees it and believes it might be her sister. She calls police, her DNA is compared to the remains, and it matches. That right there is what you call a "hit," no two ways about it.

After doing the job for more than a decade, I was always happy to hear about hits and arrests from cold cases, but I didn't go out of my mind with delirious glee or post it on Facebook. An experienced forensic artist should expect a certain level of success; otherwise what are we there for?

The hits never happen in a nice, predictable succession anyway. Sometimes I could go a full year without a peep, then three or four cases might get cleared within a month's time. It's the roller-coaster nature of the work.

I never got too wrapped up in how my facial approximations were resolved. If the family hadn't seen the sculpture, and the identification came as a result of the FBI's national DNA database, fine. If my sculpture bore a resemblance to the person, I'd be pleased. Of course, I would always be thrilled with a spot-on resemblance. Who wouldn't be? It's an exhilarating feeling, and flattering when the detectives remark on it.

But too much praise makes me uncomfortable. I'm not trying to be all "aw shucks" while kicking my shoe in the dirt. I know it sounds corny, but I really am just doing my job. What I really cared about was learning from it. What errors in judgment did I make, and were they avoidable? What did I do right, and could I draw any conclusions to use in my next case?

That said, I'll never forget my first official identification. It was my second sculpture ever, and it's what you would call a perfect hit—not counting the quality of the sculpting.

I'll explain. It was a Saturday, and I was out pumping gas when my cell phone rang. It was Wade.

"Hey, did you hear what happened?"

I thought he was talking about something at work. As I started grumbling, he interrupted me and said, "No dummy, you got a hit."

"What are you talking about? How do you know I got a hit, and I don't?"

"Well, I'm trying to tell you now if you'd just shut up and listen! I'm at the anthropology conference, and the detective just called Chris.

The sculpture had been shown on the local news, and the police got a call. A couple had been watching, and the wife thought it looked a bit like her sister-in-law. The man looked, and yes, it did look a bit like her. He listened to the report, and there were physical traits that fit too. He called the police and said, "I think that might be my sister."

She had been out of contact with the family for years and was never reported missing. There was some trouble with the law, a few stints in jail, and a history of addiction. He gave a DNA sample, and sure enough, it was a match.

Every artist remembers their first hit, and I'll never forget that one. I was elated. *Oh my God! I can't believe it. It worked! I helped! I know what I'm doing!* And then I immediately felt guilty. *How can I be happy? I am being awful, aren't I?*

But Reid pointed out the obvious: "You aren't happy thinking about what the family is going through, and you certainly aren't happy about her death. You are happy that you have validation."

I had worked for years to learn facial approximation, and now there was bona fide success. I had been part of a team that had resulted in the successful resolution of a cold case, and now maybe the police could get one step closer to finding out who killed her.

Of course, when I saw her picture, I was unhappy all over again. There actually was a resemblance, but the sculpture? Ugh. It was slightly better than my very first, but not by much. There were so many things I hadn't figured out yet. I needed a sculpting instructor, someone who was a hell of a lot better than me who could point out my errors and show me how to do things right.

I wanted the absolute best. My criterion was that their work be utterly realistic. I was trying to bring my sculptures to life and make them believable as a real person so they would be taken seriously. I knew I might never make it, because most of the sculptors had twenty years of experience under their belts and I was just starting. But hey, I wanted a challenge.

You'd be amazed at how hard it is to find a portrait instructor. There was no lack of phenomenal sculptors; the problem was they were so phenomenal that either they were too busy to teach or all their classes were sold out a year in advance.

The artist I would have cut off a limb to study with was Jeni Fairey. Her work was jaw-droppingly beautiful and astoundingly realistic. She had been a primary sculptor at Madame Tussauds, and had created the faces of Simon Cowell, Tupac Shakur, and even Queen Elizabeth. Her skill practically brought tears to my eyes, and even though I knew I'd never be able to get that accomplished in a thousand lifetimes, I knew studying with her would help me get closer.

She had classes listed on her website, but no schedule, so I emailed her to ask about training. She wrote a very kind note back explaining that she was taking time off for family and might be back to teaching in a year or so.

Nothing if not determined, I set an email reminder to myself for exactly one year in the future. When the alert dinged 365 days later, I wrote back to her. The message was something along the lines of "I don't mean to be a pushy American, but it's been a year, and I was wondering if you were back to teaching yet?"

That started a conversation, and over the course of a few weeks we worked out the logistics. I would come and study with her, one-on-one, for three days, in her studio. I was thrilled beyond words, and put in my request for training the very next day.

All FBI employees are required to get at least fifteen hours of training every year, so this would cover me. I didn't expect cost to be a factor, since it would be less than other classes I had taken in the past. That's why I was surprised when my request came back the next day from Harry: Denied.

His reason? "Not Mission Critical."

That was ludicrous. At least 70 percent of my assigned work was sculpting; how could that be anything *but* mission critical?

I went to his office for a sit-down.

"This is some really important training. I've never had any formal sculpting training, I'm all self-taught."

"Well, you got an ID with your last sculpture, so what you're doing must be OK."

"Maybe it was OK, but OK isn't good enough. We're supposed to be better than that. I mean, this is the FBI. Plus, Jack went to two conferences, and he's only a probationary employee."

I knew that wouldn't go over well, but I had to say it. Probationary employees were never sent to outside training, especially when it came with a high price tag. It was simply unheard of, and it made sense. Why spend money training a person when you don't know if they'll make it through the year? As it turns out, Harry wasted thousands of dollars on Jack; he was fired a month after this conversation.

"These sculptures are for unidentified victims; they need to be as good as they can be. It's like their last chance at being identified."

He scoffed. "There's nothing in the FBI that says unidentified people are part of our mission."

"Harry, it's *literally* carved into the rock in front of the laboratory."

"That doesn't mean it's part of our mission. The answer is still no."

OK, so *this* is how it's going to be? It's bad enough that I wasn't allowed to have the software I needed and my BlackBerry and laptop had been taken away. Now, I can't even get training, even after all the guys in the unit have gone? Money wasn't the issue; there was plenty in the budget. This was just one more instance of Harry and Frank treating me like a second-class employee and holding me back from my work.

I vented to Reid when I got home.

"Fuck them. Go anyway," was his response. We had just bought a house, so it's not like we had money coming out of our ears, but Reid was insistent.

Two months later, I was sitting next to Jeni Fairey, in her rose-covered studio. (Seriously, it's like out of a fairytale.) As it turns out, we had a lot in common. She and I were both nervous fliers, she was a vegetarian like me, had a cat named Daisy (me too!), and we both shared an affinity for dark chocolate and red wine. If that's not the basis for a nice friendship, I don't know what is.

One day while she was demonstrating a sculpting technique, I mentioned a video I had seen about ten years before. "I think it was about Madame Tussaud's. It was all about how they create those sculptures of celebrities. It was so cool!"

Jeni kept working as I talked. I could see she had an odd expression on her face, but I didn't catch on.

"Then they showed the sculpture next to the person, and I swear you couldn't even tell which one was real and which one was clay! I wish I could remember where I saw it or who it was about. I'd buy it just so I could watch it again."

Very quietly, Jeni said, "That was me."

"What?" I said, still a bit clueless.

"In the documentary. That was me. I was the sculptor."

"Get out! Serious? That's crazy!!"

I couldn't believe the coincidence. Way before I ever thought I'd be in the FBI, and before I ever gave a thought to sculpting, I had seen this documentary, completely agog at the artist's skill, and now I was in her studio, two feet away from her, sculpting. I felt it was meant to be.

10

Of Course, You Know This Means War

One morning, Carol Dobbs from the Office of Public Affairs called me to her office. Besides being a lawyer, she was an FBI agent and part of the front office as far as hierarchy goes.

"So, let's talk about this *Dateline* episode you're going to be on. We have a request from an agency that's asking us to redo a reconstruction that was done a few years ago. They got some leads but no hits, so they're sending in the skull to have it redone."

This was news to me. I hadn't heard anything about my being on an episode of *Dateline*.

"Oh, OK. Harry didn't say anything to me about it, but sure." Even though Harry was my supervisor, as he so often reminded me, Carol outranked him by a mile. If Carol said I was going to be on *Dateline*, then by golly, I was going to be on *Dateline*.

To be honest, I would rather hide under a desk than be on TV. I hate having my picture taken and even skipped my high school senior portrait, which my mother never forgave me for. But when the Office of Public Affairs picks you as the person who is going to represent the FBI in an interview, that's what you do.

I liked Carol. We'd known each other a couple years by now, and I had taken part in other interviews with her by my side. Whenever an FBI employee is interviewed, there is always a representative from public affairs there. It's not as though they don't trust the employee to know their job, but rather it's for the employee's (and FBI's) protection. You never know what a reporter is going to ask, and the public affairs officer is there to intervene if a question is inappropriate or off-limits.

I don't know anything about the Russia investigation or Hillary's emails, and between you, me, and the lamppost, I don't really care. But things get misreported all the time—not for any agency misdeeds or media conspiracy, but because shit happens.

Case in point: I was out gardening one weekend when Carol called me asking, "Have you ever taken any casework skulls home?"

That's like asking if . . . well, if you've ever stored actual human skulls in your living room.

"Oh my God, no!" I said, horrified at the question.

"I didn't think so," Carol replied calmly. "But I've got the draft here of the article you were interviewed for. Where in the world did the reporter get that idea, I wonder?"

I was wondering too. It was so out of left field.

"The only skull in my house is the one my husband gave me for Christmas, and it's fake. I might've told her about that."

"OK, don't worry, I just had to make sure."

If you've ever wondered why FBI employees come off so stiff and robotic in interviews, this is why. It's hard to act natural when you are trying your level best not to slip up or mangle your words. We always need to be hyperaware of what we're saying and how we say it, lest our words get misconstrued or taken out of context. That was a crisis averted, thanks to FBI policy.

Carol was going to be with me on the interview for *Dateline* too, so she started to fill me in on the case. As she talked, a bell of recognition rang in my head.

"Wait, is this one from Arizona? Does she have short, curly dark hair?"

"Yes, how'd you know that?"

"Well, I'd like to say I'm some kind of genius, but really, most forensic artists follow other cases. We do Google alerts for skulls and unidentified remains, the whole nine yards. They just stick in your head for whatever reason, and this one really did, especially because I know the artist."

Carol asked, "Then why does this guy want it redone?"

"Because a lot of people just don't understand how facial approximation works. That sculpture has only been out two years, it's simply a matter of the right person not seeing it yet. If she didn't have any family or close friends, then the right person may never see it. She may never be identified, that's how it is."

"Wow, that's so sad," Carol said. "I had no idea."

"Can I use your computer? I can look it up and see if that's the one."

It didn't take long to find it.

"Please, Carol, don't make me redo it. I know it'd be nice for the FBI to be featured on *Dateline*, but it can't be on this case. There's nothing I would do different at all."

"No, of course not. Well, thank goodness. That could have been very embarrassing."

I walked back to my office gritting my teeth. All this could have been prevented if Harry had simply asked the contributor more about the case before accepting it. Like he was supposed to.

When an agency requests an approximation, we are supposed to ask them a number of questions, the first one being, "Has an approximation been done for this skull before? That's because the FBI laboratory

isn't in the business of redoing another agency's work. This is especially true for DNA and fingerprints, because if the case goes to court,
the defense attorney could insinuate that the police were "shopping
around" for the laboratory results they wanted.

The only time an approximation is accepted for a do-over is if there
is a valid reason that brings something new to the case that wasn't
available before. For instance, if the artist had done a 2D drawing
fifteen years ago, then you could make the argument that the 3D
rendition might be more accurate, given the advances in the field, or
generate enough media attention to get viable leads. There have also
been times where DNA showed that the remains weren't female, as
previously thought, but male. Then it's definitely time for a do-over.

It was bad enough that Carol had to call the agency and renege on
accepting the case, but there was also the matter of the skull. Harry
had already told the agency to send it, so it was winging its way to
Quantico that very moment.

This whole episode, the waste of time and resources, made what
happened the next day even more galling.

Before you read this next part, I'm going to encourage you to pour
yourself a glass of wine (or the beverage of your choice) and suspend
disbelief, because what happens next is so over the top, so crazy, it
doesn't seem like it could ever happen in a professional workplace,
much less the FBI. But it did happen. There was another person in
the room when it was happening, a room full of people outside the
office who heard it while it was happening, and three signed sworn
statements afterward saying, "Yes, this happened just as Lisa said it
did, and I'm signing my name to it."

As these horror stories so often start, my phone rang, and the call
was from Harry. "Come into my office now. And bring Wade."

He was already wound up when we walked in. Wade and I looked at each other, not knowing what was going on. Usually, Harry had Frank right by his side for everything, but Frank was out that day, and apparently Harry couldn't wait one more minute to humiliate me.

Swiveling his chair toward me like a detective in a B movie, he asked, "Why did Carol talk to you yesterday, and not me? I'm the supervisor."

Uh-oh, whenever he reminds us that he's the supervisor, things won't go well.

Cautiously, I said, "I don't know. There was a voicemail from her to come to her office, so I did."

"But why did she call you?"

"Harry, I don't know. She left the message on my voicemail to see her right away, so I did."

"But I still don't get why she's calling you and not me. She needs to talk to me! I'm the supervisor!" He was getting angrier now, his voice rising.

"I know, but she's an agent. She's sort of got rank here."

"Well, I'm the supervisor, not you. She should've called me," he grumbled. "Why didn't she?"

I was trying not to show my exasperation at the ridiculousness of the conversation, so I shrugged and said, "It beats me, really. I don't know."

"What do you mean you don't know? Maybe you just don't *want* to know."

What does that even mean? I just stayed silent at this point, because answering him was exhausting and he wasn't paying attention anyway. Brick walls were more receptive.

"Answer me, why did she call you and not me?"

"Harry, I don't know what more you want me to say. You've asked me, and I've answered. I don't know why she called me and not you."

Now, Harry started chuckling and said, "You don't need to keep repeating yourself. You just keep saying the same thing over and over. You don't need to keep on repeating yourself."

"But you're asking me the same question, so all I can do is answer it the same. Maybe ask Carol why, because I have no idea."

It was obvious he was itching for a fight and doing all he could to be confrontational. This back-and-forth had been going on a good five minutes, and I was exhausted from trying to get through to him. It was pointless—there was no reason for him to come after me like this other than pure venom.

It occurred to me that maybe Carol had chewed him out a bit for blindsiding her and wasting her time, and now he was taking it out on me. After all, she had put in a fair amount of work setting the whole thing up and had spoken to the producers at length discussing what they wanted. A crew would come down to the laboratory and film me during the sculpture process, and then the final sculpture would be unveiled at the end of the show. It would have been great TV. Except Harry managed to botch it, embarrassing Carol in the process.

Harry changed course and demanded, "Why did you think you were going to be the one doing the reconstruction? I had already assigned that to Wade."

"I *didn't* think I was going to be doing it. I didn't even know anything about it until Carol called me in. I have no control over what cases I get, especially when it comes from public affairs."

"You're always doing stuff like this, getting big cases. Wade needs to have some high-profile cases to work on too, you know."

"Like I said, case assignments aren't up to me. I have no problem with Wade doing it."

That triggered something in Harry. "I didn't say you had a problem with it! Did I say you had a problem with it? Did I?"

This was getting more infuriating and humiliating by the moment. No matter what I said or how I said it, it was wrong. He started puffing up, rising out of his chair, "Answer me. Did I? Did I say you had a problem with it?"

In my best Stepford-wife monotone, I said, "No, Harry, I didn't say that you had a problem with it. It was just a manner of speaking."

"Well, it sure sounded like you had a problem with it."

"Again, there was never a problem, it was just a manner of speaking."

Harry's face lit up with delight as he started chuckling. "Now, you're not making any sense! You're just going on and on and not making any sense at all!" He was really enjoying himself now, especially my inability to say anything to defend myself.

He kept laughing and rocking in his chair while I had to sit there and take it. "Nope, you're not making any sense at all! You just keep on babbling! This is all you're doing."

To illustrate his point, he raised his arms in the air, shook his hands over his head like he was waving imaginary butterflies away, wiggled his fingers, rolled his eyes, and laughed as he said, "This is you!" There followed nonsensical gibberish noises: "*Blip, bloop, bloop, bloop!* I don't know! I don't know! Hahahahaha! *Bloop, bloop, bloop!* This is you!"

My rage at this point was indescribable. My fingers were gripping the edge of the chair, and I narrowed my eyes watching him. *You son of a bitch.* I wasn't afraid of him; I absolutely hated him. I despised his smug face, his stupidity, and his sheer meanness. He was reveling in his power, bullying a subordinate when he knew there wasn't anything I could do about it. Two years ago, we had been friends, coworkers, went out on cases together, and now this.

My face was hot with fury and embarrassment, but I didn't say a word. I couldn't. He'd take any movement or word from me as insubordination, which he would instantly report to Frank. I sat as still as I possibly could but had no control over my flared nostrils and gritted teeth. Wade looked as though he wanted to melt into the floorboards. I know he was embarrassed and mad for my sake, but he was as helpless as I was to do anything.

What's a person to do when faced with someone who is clearly off the rails, and that someone is your supervisor? I was embarrassed and furious and prayed that he would tire himself out like a screaming child having a tantrum. I just sat there and kept my mouth shut, my nails digging into my palms.

The silence went on forever. Finally, finally, finally he waved his hand and said, "You're dismissed."

I couldn't open the door fast enough. Wade walked next to me saying quietly, "It's OK, it's OK. Let's just get back to the office, and we'll all talk. It's OK."

We walked past the cubicles where the photographers, who had heard everything, were trying to pretend they hadn't. Ted knew something was very wrong the second we walked in. For a moment, I just stood there, vibrating with rage. There's a part in *Gone with the Wind* (the book, not the movie) where Scarlett is seething with anger and frustration. I'll never forget how Margaret Mitchell put it: her description was "a small fiend with a pair of hot tweezers plucked behind Scarlett's eyeballs." That. Was. Me. I didn't have a water pitcher handy like Scarlett did, and without thinking threw my glasses on the floor and walked out.

I went down the hall and just paced and paced and tried to collect myself. There was no way on God's green earth I was going to cry, I was too pissed off with righteous anger. I went back to my desk and called the EEO counselor. This shit was going to stop right now.

On Monday morning, we were thrilled to find out that Harry was going to be out of the office for three whole days. Frank didn't say why, and we didn't care. Any time Harry was gone was A-OK by us.

On Thursday morning, who should walk into our office but Harry, all bright eyed and bushy tailed, wearing a smile and carrying a box of donuts. Wade, Ted, and I were all exchanging suspicious glances, as if to say, *Does he think we can be bought this easily?*

Harry made it a point to not look at me, and I'm sure in his mind all was forgiven. He was attempting to make small talk with us, like we had all been BFFs, and it was falling flat. After this went on way too long, he turned to me and Wade, and said we needed to follow him into Frank's office.

We dutifully traipsed behind, and then sat for an incredibly awkward exchange that entailed Harry sitting ramrod straight in a chair with his hands on his knees as he apologized for his behavior of the previous week.

"I would like to say that I am sorry for my actions. You might have wondered why I was out the past three days. It was to attend leadership training. Please bear with me as I learn to be a better supervisor."

Well, *that* didn't sound rehearsed at all!

Frank nodded, and with his insincere, termite smile said, "Let's just put all that's happened behind us and start over. It's all water under the bridge."

Water under the bridge, my eye. I already had set up an appointment with Grace, and I wasn't about to cancel it for some lame apology. I was fully determined to start the official process and request mediation.

I was allowed to go straight to filing a formal EEO complaint, but that isn't looked upon favorably by the administrative judge, who is the person who will be hearing the case. Every agency has to report the number of complaints they get each year and make them public, and I'm sure the FBI wants to keep their record spotless. How else can they brag that they have a zero-tolerance policy against discrimination?

In mediation, the employee would sit down with the supervisor in a neutral setting, with an unbiased mediator who would guide the talk. It's like family therapy. The employee states what they want, such as "Please stop yelling at me and sabotaging my casework," and the supervisors respond and say what they want.

If an agreement can be reached, the terms are spelled out very distinctly, no vague language that someone can wiggle out of. Then everyone signs it, including the mediator, and DR. HUBERT BUNSEN, the director of the laboratory. This is now a legally binding agreement that the FBI must adhere to.

Grace was appropriately horrified at what I told her, but now there was a problem. Because Harry had gone to training, apologized, and promised to be a better supervisor, going forward with mediation would be like a moot point to the FBI. After all, isn't better treatment and an apology what I wanted? It could backfire, and I would come across as the agitator.

I was crestfallen, not that I was looking forward to starting an EEO complaint. I knew that I could be opening myself up to a whole world of hurt even mentioning the possibility. But is this how the system really worked? They could get away with it that easily?

The whole hideous situation felt like being in an abusive relationship. Now, I had to wait until Harry and Frank did something even more awful to me before I could request mediation.

———————

Besides all this, I had some serious family issues to contend with. My mom, who was eighty-six at the time, was in an assisted living facility just a few miles from my home, and I often had to take family leave to take her to doctor appointments or handle emergencies.

One emergency was particularly ghastly. She had been getting on the assisted living facility's bus to go to lunch, when she slipped and broke her ankle. *Backward.* It's almost a blessing that she had neuropathy in her legs, but her foot had literally done a 180 and was facing the wrong direction. Now, she was in the emergency room confused, distraught, and asking for me. She was in a lot of pain, and she was scared. And when your mom needs you, you are there.

Maybe Harry was raised by wolves, since that's the only explanation for what happened next. If an employee is out of the office owing to a family emergency, especially something this bad, there's no telling when they would be back. I told Harry that I would be out of the office indefinitely and would keep him updated on the situation.

When I got back to work after an exhausting week dealing with doctors and hospitals and a mother in pain, I found out that Harry had assigned me a postmortem retouch, and it was due in two days.

Now, there's several things wrong with this. First off, postmortem retouches are never given a two-day turnaround, unless it's something like the terrorist-heads-in-a-bucket case. Otherwise, by definition, postmortem retouches are cold cases. Like everyone else in the world, forensic artists prioritize their work based on what is more urgently needed, and what can be put further down the to-do list. Given our typical workload, a reasonable turnaround for a postmortem retouch is two to three weeks. That's because artists need to gather more information, things that aren't always sent in when the case is first submitted. Most often, we only receive one image, but 90 percent of the time there are more available; the detective just might not have realized we wanted them.

Before we begin a postmortem retouch, we always ask the investigating officer for all other photos that are available of the victim. Having the crime scene photos, and the morgue photos, both before and after the victim has been cleaned by the medical examiner, gives us every possible angle of the victim's face to work with. There are always photos of the victim after the body has been rinsed off, but we might be able to glean the person's hairstyle from the crime scene photos before the hair is wet and slicked back.

We also need to have a copy of the medical examiner's report. That's where the information about sex, stature, race, and estimated age will be. The medical examiner will also have noted particular things about the person, like "dark raised moles on left cheek." If the artist didn't know that ahead of time, those moles could look like dried blood droplets, and we might unintentionally remove an identifying feature.

Even with multiple photos, postmortem facial approximations are extremely challenging, because of the amount of trauma the body has been through. It can be difficult to determine the face shape with any certainty on account of bloating, from either trauma or decomposition. The way the person died, and even the position at the time of death, will affect the face. Dead people do not look like they're sleeping, even if they happened to have died in their sleep. The image of your great aunt Edna lying peacefully in a coffin is a kindness made possible by the skilled hands of a mortician.

If a person died face down, not only will the facial features be distorted, but the blood will also pool and settle, giving the face a mottled, dark purple appearance. This is what's known as lividity, and lots of TV detectives solve crimes this way. The credit goes to the real-life medical examiner, who can tell if a body has been moved because the lividity pattern doesn't jibe with the way the body was found. If a person is found lying on his back, but the face is dark purply red, that's an indication that the body had been flipped over while the person was still alive. A person who died on his back and stays that way would have a pale face, drained of color, because gravity would have made the blood pool to the back of the head and body.

Even in a natural death, there's plenty of work to be done. But the majority of the cases we deal with are homicides, so there are most likely going to be bruises, severe cuts, or even bullet wounds on the face to deal with. Remains that have spent an extended time in water will be bloated, and often completely bald. Even the eyebrows and lashes are gone.

As the body bloats, the hair follicles lose their grip on the surrounding tissue and fall out, lost to the river or pool of water they were found in. So, while we've lost any indication of hair length or style, at least we can tell where the hairline and eyebrows were because of the textural differences in the skin.

Eye color is distorted too. The corneas cloud over, and depending on the temperature, humidity, and air movement, blue eyes could alter to appear reddish brown, or brown eyes may be covered with a film that makes them look bluish gray. Death doesn't literally turn your brown eyes blue, but it can certainly appear that way.

Even if there is no trauma to the face, there's still a lot of work that goes into a retouch to make it suitable for release to the public. Generally, the eyes are only half-open or completely closed. The mouth has usually fallen open, because the muscles that keep it closed (temporalis and masseter) no longer work. So we need to digitally open their eyes and close their mouth without distorting the shape of their face.

A morgue photo isn't usually taken at a normal angle as if it were a portrait, because the body is lying on its back. The best a medical examiner can do is to tilt the exam table to place the decedent in a more upright position and take the photo that way. If the person has been autopsied, a sheet will be wrapped around the head to hide the fact that the cranium has been sawed open to collect brain tissue. When only the face is visible, we need to recreate the neck and hair too.

That's why postmortem approximations can be very time consuming and are often the most difficult cases a forensic artist can work on. Our job is to do the forensic version of what mortuary specialists do. We digitally heal the broken bones, bullet wounds, and decomposition on the face of the dead in order to reanimate the face and make it appropriate for release to the public.

It is also the last-ditch effort to identify a body. As I've said, nobody is going to suggest removing the head for an approximation. After a certain amount of time in storage at the morgue, the body will be buried, and that's it.

When I first saw the case assignment, I was irritated. There was absolutely no reason for this case to have been escalated to an urgent status. Not only was the case well over nine months old, but the man also committed suicide. This is obviously very sad, but there was no urgency here.

I tried to give Harry the benefit of the doubt. Maybe there was some reason it was marked urgent, so I went to his office to talk about it.

"Harry, can I ask about this postmortem? Is there a press conference or something scheduled?"

"No."

Huh, OK. If there had been, then that would be a reason for upping the priority. Once the media is interested in a case, you want to jump on the opportunity as fast as you can.

"Do you know why the detective wants it in two days then? Is there a potential ID where he wants to show the family a sanitized version of the image or something?"

The days of showing ravaged, mutilated bodies to a sobbing family member for a positive identification are gone, if that even happened. I only think it did because I saw it on TV.

"No. I emailed you about this case when you were gone. I told him you could have it done in two days. That's plenty of time."

Harry set the deadline? No, no, no, that's not how it works. This is how it works: the detective will ask, "How long does something like this take anyway?" and we'll say, "Barring any unforeseen circumstances, two to three weeks is a normal turnaround. If you need it sooner than that, we'll do what we can to get it to you."

"Harry, how could I have known about it when you emailed me? I don't have a BlackBerry, remember?"

"Well, I told you about it before you left."

"No, Harry, you didn't. I didn't even know when I'd be back, because my mother was in the emergency room. She had a really bad accident."

"No, I did tell you, and two days is plenty of time. Just get it done."

"But I don't even have the medical examiner's report, or any other photos to go on. I need that before I can start."

To make matters even worse, there was a four-hour "all-hands" meeting scheduled the next day. These are incredibly boring, redundant time sucks, because all the speakers do is read the bullet points from PowerPoint presentations and tell us things that we already knew or could easily look up: make sure you lock your safe at the end of the day, don't talk about cases outside of the office, blah blah blah. The entire event is videotaped for anyone who can't attend owing to their workload, thus reiterating the FBI's mantra "casework always comes first."

Given this, I asked Harry if I could be excused and watch the video later.

"No. This is a mandatory meeting. I told you. You should have planned your time better. I'll let you stay late to get it done."

Oh, you'll let me. Gee, thanks.

I didn't even bother responding. I went to the stupid meeting, tapping my foot the whole time, and started back on the retouch so I could get it done before 3:30 PM. Frank had instituted a policy where he and Harry both insisted on "quality-checking" every item Wade and I worked on before it was sent back to the requester. This is micromanagement on an absurd level, because Frank knew nothing whatsoever about forensic art, and Harry was a close second. Frank never checked the photographer's work, so this was clearly a demeaning exercise that he saved for the forensic artists.

"Harry, I'm almost done. Can you look at it so I can send it to the detective?

"No, I don't have time now. I'm going home."

So much for the importance of checking my work. When it's 3:30, Harry bolts out the door like his hair is on fire.

Great, here I am staying late to work on a supposedly urgent case, but apparently, it's not important enough for Harry to stay at work and check it per his own rules? I had held myself in check during all this, because I needed to focus and get the job done. I couldn't afford to give in to anger and dwell on how ridiculous and infuriating the entire situation was. A manufactured "emergency" for no other reason than spite, to the detriment of the victim. I blocked out everything going on around me and worked with laser focus.

But after? After I finished the retouch and called the detective, and after I got in my car to make the drive home? My mind was made up.

Harry had crossed a line that should never have been crossed. It was one thing to come after me. Heck, I've stayed late at work plenty of times. But now he was playing with other people's lives, a young man lying in a morgue unidentified, and a family who had no idea what happened to their son or brother. They all deserved better.

I did the best I could with the image and the tools I had at the time, but it never should have come to that in the first place. You don't fuck with victims. Fine, go ahead, screw with me and make my life miserable, but to take it out on victims? It was beyond the pale. It was petty and evil, and it was my very last straw.

I thought of my dad and what he would think. And I thought again of his words of wisdom and knew I was doing the right thing: "There is a certain amount of horseshit you have to put up with in this world. Just don't let anybody rub your face in it."

Even though I had talked to Mr. Bean about Harry and Frank's conduct several times before, I truly thought that once everything was out in the open, the front office would understand how bad the situation was and would do something about them both.

The FBI touts mediation as a very efficient process that saves time and money, and at that point I actually believed it. In reality, mediation is a bit like *Fight Club*: the first rule of mediation is, you do not talk about mediation. Anything you say during the process can go no further. Participants are restricted from using their BlackBerry (not that I had one) to look anything up or take notes, and we weren't even allowed to keep paper notes. Everything had to be destroyed after the meeting.

Employees are allowed to have a lawyer present, but the mediator gets to decide how much input the attorney can have and can even prevent them from speaking. Since mediations were said to take three to four hours, I didn't see the point of spending $1,500 to $2,000 for an attorney when all they might be able to do is sit there and watch.

Grace assured me that any agreement reached was legally binding. I was afraid that I would go through the whole process for nothing, that we'd come up with an agreement and then the FBI would never follow through. After many discussions, Grace insisted that I would be safe and that the FBI had a legal obligation to abide by the agreement.

When you enter mediation, you need to have a goal in mind. All I wanted was to get the hell out of the Photo Unit. I didn't want to go back to the Graphic Unit, because Brent was still there. Management had never showed any interest in keeping him away from me. I had tried to make them set boundaries, but he always had free rein.

I didn't want to keep looking over my shoulder and worry about getting pummeled every day, so the unit I'd ask to go to would be the Science Unit. It made perfect sense, because that's where the forensic anthropologists worked, and it would be more efficient for everyone involved when working on facial approximations.

I knew I was in trouble within minutes of the meeting starting. The mediator walked in wearing a red-and-white college lanyard around his neck, and by some strange coincidence, Harry happened to have graduated from that very same school! So my fair and neutral process began with Harry and the mediator regaling each other with jokes and memories from the good old days at ol' So-and-So State.

Harry was accompanied by KATHY MORNINGSIDE, deputy assistant director of the FBI laboratory. She was second in command, with the authority to sign the agreement, so her signature was as good as Dr. Bunsen's. What I didn't expect was that she would be Harry's mouthpiece. She sat next to him, and across from me, a classic confrontational setup, and sided with him every step of the way.

I wish I could say that the mediation took three to four hours; it lasted almost nine. I wish I could say it felt fair and neutral. But the mediator continued to be chatty with Harry during the breaks, and Kathy made excuses for Harry all day long. The kicker was when she rationalized that Harry's actions weren't evidence of discrimination but incompetence.

"If Harry delays your casework or assigns you a job without sufficient time to complete it," she reasoned, "it's not discrimination. It's his lack of ability as a supervisor."

Only Harry could sit there with a smug look on his face while being roundly insulted.

My requested transfer to the Science Unit was given a hard no. "That's not happening," Kathy said rigidly. No negotiation, period. Finally, at the bitter end to a long, exhausting, and frustrating day, it was agreed that I would go back to the Graphic Unit. Of course, that wasn't my first choice, but at least it was something. I had the FBI's word, in writing, that I was getting out of the Photo Unit.

When the executive management of the foremost law enforcement agency in the world gives you it's word, in writing, that they will protect you, even the most cynical person could be excused for believing. And for a time, I believed.

I wasn't supposed to say anything after mediation, so I didn't. Sooner or later, everyone would know when my computer was moved to the Graphic Unit. I had two weeks to get my casework together and clean up my desk for the move downstairs. I didn't think much of the email that came the next week. "Please come to my office to go over the terms of your mediation," Kathy wrote. Yay! It was really happening.

"As you know," Kathy said, "under the terms of the mediation agreement, you will be transferred to the Graphic Unit." She paused. "But your work area won't be down there. You'll stay at the desk you have now."

"I'm sorry? I don't understand."

"You are being administratively transferred to the Graphic Unit. But you will still physically sit in the Photo Unit, at the desk you have now."

It took a moment for that to sink in. "I have to stay up there with Harry and Frank?"

"Yes."

"But why? The agreement said I'd go back to Graphics. Why can't I be with the rest of my unit?"

Kathy started fidgeting in her chair, "Well, it's . . . it's a personnel issue."

Here it comes again. Knowing the answer before I asked, I said, "Brent."

After a very long pause, she owned up to it. "Yes."

There it was. Perfect. I have to stay in a room fifteen feet away from the men yelling at me all day and sabotaging my casework because of the other guy who wants to break my face? Got it.

"But I have to ask," Kathy continued. "Why would you be willing to go back there, I mean . . . aren't you worried?"

"Well, sure, a little. But I can take a punch if I have to. At least I'd still have a job. Harry and Frank have been trying to fire me for years. They just make up all this stuff up and—"

"Shush!" Kathy quickly put her hands up. "Stop! We don't need to get into that again."

Whenever there's talk of discrimination and reprisal against women, the party line is always, "We need more women in management!" Women, they say, are more aware of discrimination because they've probably had their share in the workplace, and thus they are more likely to stick up for their fellow female workmates.

Kathy had heard every single hideous detail about my life in the Photo Unit during the mediation, and she wasn't doing a damn thing about it. She was one step below Dr. Bunsen, the laboratory director, she had the power to help me, but she chose to sit on her hands. And I'd say it's worked out quite well for her. In 2016 Barack Obama bestowed her with a Presidential Rank Award, and two years after that she was honored for her work as a Leadership Fellow in the International Women's Forum.

Thanks for all you do on behalf of women in the workplace, Kathy!

The day before I was supposed to be transferred to the Graphic Unit (on paper, at least), I was summoned to Bunsen's office. He was sitting at the head of a conference table, holding my mediation agreement, and Felicia Gruel, the human resources unit chief, was sitting on his right. Uh-oh.

"I'm not going to honor this agreement. You can either stay in the Photo Unit and report to Frank or file a formal complaint. But you're not going to Graphics."

I felt like I had been hit in the head with a brick. I guess at this point I should have expected something underhanded like this, but I had sincerely put my trust in the FBI. Their zero-tolerance stance on anything related to harassment, bullying, and discrimination had been drilled into our heads for years.

"But why?" I asked. "It was all agreed. It's in writing."

"It's a personnel issue."

He wouldn't even say his name, the coward.

"You mean Brent, don't you?"

Bunsen nodded.

I tried to take all this information in before asking, "So why can't I go to the Science Unit? That's where the anthropologists are, and I work with them. It makes sense."

"No," he said, without hesitation. "I'm not about to have an artist in that unit."

Since when are forensic artists the black sheep in law enforcement? I had a drawer full of attaboys and thank-you letters from agents for my work, and even from Bunsen himself. It was infuriating to be seen as a lower form of life because I didn't have "Dr." in front of my name.

"But having me report directly to Frank won't do any good, he's worse than Harry. He's the real problem here, why can't you do something about him?"

That's when Felicia chirped helpfully, "You could always quit and get another job!"

My head swiveled around to face her. "I'm a fifty-year-old forensic artist, and the FBI is the only federal agency that has an effort dedicated solely to facial approximations. Where else am I supposed to go? And why do I have to be the one to leave? I'm not the one who's done anything wrong. Harry and Frank are the ones who are breaking the law."

She clammed up, with a shocked expression that I had dared to point out the obvious. I looked to Bunsen for his response, but he just sat there, staring at me blankly.

"Please, I can't stay there. I've done everything I'm supposed to, I followed all the rules—"

He cut me off. "Either stay in the Photo Unit and report directly to Frank or file a formal complaint. You have until tomorrow to decide."

I remember going back to my sculpting room, pacing, feeling like a trapped animal. Who could I call? Where could I go for help? Dr. Bunsen has a boss, doesn't he? Maybe I could go to them.

But the only person above Bunsen's head was Robert Mueller, and good luck getting to him. He's like the Wizard of Oz. No way, no how, would I ever be granted an audience. I could try emailing him, but he'd never see it; his "people" would. I know this because a friend of mine tried. She had been going through her own particular hell, wrote to the director in desperation, and let's just say it didn't go well for her. It was considered insubordination to jump the chain of command, even though she had gone through every link of that chain and hit a brick wall.

Then it hit me. *The agency ombudsman, JANET HOFFMAN! She has a direct line to him!* She said so in that stupid town-hall meeting I had to go to. I called Janet with a glimmer of hope.

"I'm sorry. That's not something I can talk to the director about," she replied. "You've already entered the EEO process."

"But I never wanted to enter the EEO process in the first place! You said we could come to you. You said you could go to the director with anything."

"I'm sorry. My hands are tied."

The FBI reminds us all the time that the EEO process is there for our benefit. "We're zero-tolerance, baby! The FBI is a family, and we don't put up with any of that nonsense! Anybody does anything like that, they're out the door, and we mean it!"

I had done the process exactly the way I was supposed to, and look where it had gotten me. I was desperate knowing that as much as I had been abused during the past two years, it was only going to get worse. I was a sitting duck. I had to fight back.

When I told Dr. Bunsen that I was moving forward with a formal complaint, he nodded. "You'll find all the paperwork online. And you don't need an attorney, it's simple enough to do on your own."

Right. I began looking for a lawyer the moment I got back to my desk.

OMG, you'll never guess what happened the very next day after I filed a formal complaint: I got a BlackBerry! This is the sort of thing the bureau does when confronted with wrongdoing that they can't wriggle out of. They comply way long after they should have done the right thing in the first place, then later muddy the waters and move the timeline around so they can say, "See? We gave her a BlackBerry!" Of course, it ignores the fact that they refused to issue me one for two years, but hey, what was I complaining about anyway?

I had tried to decipher all the EEO rules, but it was extremely confusing. My dad always told me, "If you don't know something there is always somebody who does, so never be too proud to ask."

I wanted advice from a lawyer, but not just anybody. It's essential to talk to someone who specializes in federal EEO law, and there's plenty of them to be found in DC. So while the FBI says you don't *have* to have a lawyer, it would be sheer lunacy for a layperson to attempt the process themselves. Every bit of communication between you and the person who will decide your fate, the EEO administrative judge, will be done through legal motions. I was thrilled to have someone on my side. Yes, I was paying out the nose, but she was worth every penny.

In order to file a formal complaint at the FBI, or any federal agency, you must have contacted an EEO counselor within forty-five days of the incident. So, let's say your supervisor has been harassing you constantly since January, and the last awful thing he did was on June 1. If you talk to an EEO counselor on July 15 about all the abuse you've been subjected to, it is viewed as an isolated incident; everything that happened before June 1 doesn't count. Worse, an isolated incident is much more likely to be brushed off, so before you dare talk to an EEO counselor you need to think long and hard about whether that incident is bad enough for them to pay attention to.

If you make the argument that all those incidents of discrimination are a "pattern of behavior," and you talked to an EEO counselor each time it happened, you are highly likely to be branded a "serial complainer," opening yourself up to disciplinary action. Yes, it is a little-known fact that if your supervisor constantly torments you, and you report each incident, you can be the one who ends up under scrutiny. It's called "abusing the EEO system," and it's an offense for which you can be fired.

So I would need to be careful about what I listed as an incident and what would be considered a pattern. This would have been impossible to do without my attorney.

I had been warned by more than one person that Frank rifled through our desks after hours. I wasn't too surprised. After all, this was the same man who stood in his office with a pair of binoculars watching people coming in and out of the laboratory. But now that he was gunning for me, I worried about the composites in my desk. What if Frank found them and decided to mess with them somehow, or even destroy one of them? I was the person responsible, so it would be my neck if anything happened.

Since composites are evidence, you might be wondering why they were in my desk in the first place. Shouldn't they be in a safe or something? Why, yes, they should! Wade and I had asked Harry several times to get one, but you can guess how that panned out. We couldn't store them in the laboratory evidence room, because it's not permanent storage; it's only meant for work coming into or out of the building for processing. Our only alternative was to keep them in a locked desk drawer, which is what we did. I stored mine in plain white three-ring binders.

That wasn't going to work in the post-EEO-complaint era though, so I decided the best place for them would be in my evidence locker. There was plenty of room, and each of us had our own combination lock. It's a sad state of affairs when you have to hide casework from your own supervisor to keep it safe, but that's the world I was living in.

One Friday when I was taking a much-needed day off, Wade called and said he needed my locker combination.

"You need it?" I asked. This is something Wade would never ask in a million years, because it's against FBI policy to give your password or combination to anyone.

In a low voice he said, "Well, I don't. Frank does."

"Oh, for Pete's sake, what for?"

"I dunno. He just said he needs to get in it, now." I could picture Frank standing outside the room with a Dixie cup to his ear listening in.

"If he needs to get in my locker so bad, why doesn't he just go to security and have them open it?" The question was mostly rhetorical, because I already knew the answer: that would leave a paper trail.

Now, I was stuck. If I didn't give Wade the combination, Frank would cite me for insubordination. But if I did give Wade the combination, Frank could get us both.

"You know I can't," I said. "He'll turn it into a security violation against us."

"I know. But you know . . . he made me ask."

"Yeah. Just tell him that I couldn't because it's against policy. I know I'll catch hell for it Monday, but whatever."

I got the surprise of my life Monday morning. I went to the unit evidence room to get one of the skulls I had been working on, and the doors to my locker were wide open. I felt like I was walking toward it in slow motion, not believing what I was seeing. It was completely empty. My skulls, my case files, everything, was gone. I did that comical, useless thing where you reach in feeling around for objects that are clearly not there and then frantically went to look for Wade.

He knew what I was about to ask the moment he saw me. "Don't worry, I've got your skulls! When I told Frank you couldn't give me your combination, he got pissed off and got bolt-cutters from the shop and tore off your lock. He and Harry took your case files. I put your skulls in my locker to keep them safe. They had just left them on the table out in the open."

This was so many kinds of wrong that I couldn't form words. Ten years of composite drawings, now with the chain of custody broken. Same goes for the skulls. The implications of that are incomprehensible to anyone who works in law enforcement. If any one of those cases ever goes to court, I wouldn't be able to testify that the evidence had been secure, from point A to point Z. Anyone could have tampered with it, and that anyone was my own boss.

"What the hell is their problem?" Wade said. He already knew, of course; Frank and Harry were on a maniacal rampage to do me in. Someone in the unit must have seen the binders in my locker and snitched to Frank about them, probably hoping for a pat on the head and a biscuit.

Evidently, Frank's angle was to hit me with a security violation for improperly storing nonevidentiary items, because I was called into his office moments later. My case files were on the floor where they had been dumped unceremoniously the Friday before, sitting in an unlocked office all weekend. Frank was at his desk looking triumphant, and Harry sat on the couch smirking.

"Do you know why you're here?" Frank asked.

"I have an idea."

"Evidence lockers are for evidence. You are not to have anything else in them, do you understand me?

"Yes," I replied.

"This is a serious violation of FBI policy. You aren't allowed to use evidence lockers like they're your own personal bookcase. Don't you know—"

I raised my finger to speak. "Frank, those notebooks did contain evidence. They had my composites in them."

"So?"

"Composites are evidence, Frank."

I sat there and enjoyed the silence that followed. Frank didn't look like he believed me, so he looked to Harry and asked, "Is this true?"

"Yes," Harry said miserably, "it's true."

"How? They're just drawings."

"Frank," I said, "a composite is created evidence."

"That's ridiculous. I've never heard of created evidence. That can't be real."

"It's real, Frank," and I went on to explain to the man who knows everything how the composite process works.

As Ricky Gervais observed, "When you are dead, you do not know you are dead. It is only painful for others. The same applies when you are stupid."

11

Against All Odds

GRETA HUDSON was only fifteen when her mother, LILY, disappeared after a family fight in 1970. Lily had left home many times before, but this time it was different. After several days passed, the family filed a missing person's report with the Illinois police and waited.

It was twenty-six years before the family heard any news about Lily's disappearance in May 1996. Police told them that a group of hunters had stumbled upon skeletal remains in an abandoned brickyard, only three miles from the family's home. DNA analysis couldn't be performed at the time, but after reading the medical examiner's report, police felt certain it was Hudson. While some family members saw this as a closed chapter, Greta was never fully convinced that her mother was the person they buried, or that she was even dead.

In 2009 Greta persuaded investigators to reopen her mother's case after reading about advances in DNA testing and analysis. The body interred thirteen years earlier was exhumed, and DNA samples were taken for comparison with samples provided by family members. The following year, laboratory results confirmed what Greta had suspected all along: the woman they buried was not her mother after all. Could it be possible that her mother was still alive? And if this wasn't Lily, who was it?

With no DNA matches in existing databases, investigators were at a standstill in their attempt to identify the exhumed body. The remains were assigned the only name that was appropriate, Jane Doe, and given a case number, UF526. Finally, police decided that a facial approximation was the only option available. They knew that it would be a long shot. After all, the body had been unidentified for more than a decade. Was there anybody left who might even recognize her? Still, police knew they had to do something before the remains were reburied with only "Jane Doe" on the headstone. With nothing left to lose, police sent the remains of UF526 to the FBI Laboratory in Quantico, Virginia.

Occasionally, police will transport evidence to the FBI Laboratory personally, but in most cases it is sent via FedEx or another commercial carrier. There's nothing on the outside that lets drivers know what's on the inside, and that's probably for the best. Skulls, severed limbs, and even entire bodies have been shipped in for examination. Jane Doe UF526 arrived like most skeletal remains, swathed in bubble wrap inside a Styrofoam cooler, with a copy of the original police report and a request for facial approximation.

The first stop is always the anthropology department, which will examine the skull and generate a specialized report for facial approximation. This, for me, is the most important step in the process, because I can't begin work until I know the age, sex, stature, and ancestry of the person I will be reconstructing.

The anthropologist's findings are based on the amount and condition of the remains, so the more bones that are recovered, the higher the rate of accuracy. The best indication of gender is the pelvis. A female's pelvis is wider and broader than a male's, most obviously adapted for childbearing. If the pelvis wasn't recovered, the anthropologist must rely on the skull's traits and other skeletal findings to determine sex. The male skull is generally larger and more rugged, with a more substantial brow ridge, while the female skull is smoother, smaller, with a softer brow ridge. Using the skull alone, sex can be determined with only 90 percent accuracy.

Stature is best determined by measuring the femur, or thigh bone, the longest bone in the body. The anthropologist might be able to tell whether a person was stocky and muscular or smaller and more delicately framed. Bones continue to grow depending on the stress placed on them, so a bodybuilder or construction worker is going to have stronger bones and more developed muscle attachments than a piano player would.

Your skull is made up of two parts, the cranium and the mandible, consisting of twenty-two bones in total. There are eight bones to the cranium (the rounded shell consisting of the top, sides, and back of your skull) and fourteen other bones that make up your face. Obviously, your face means the eyes, which are encased by the eye orbits, nose (nasal aperture), and upper teeth (held in place by the maxilla). Your mandible is your jaw, which holds your lower teeth.

Ancestry is determined by examining the shape of the skull, along with any other remains that have been found. The anthropologist will also look at the skull for indications of age. As we get older, the sutures on our skull ossify, or fuse together, becoming more closed and less visible. The skull of a twenty-year-old is quite distinct from that of a seventy-year-old. Wear and tear on teeth also provide clues to a person's age, as well as which teeth have grown in.

Unfortunately, the findings for UF526 were maddeningly vague: Caucasian female, 4'11" to 5'4", heavyset, and fifty-five to eighty-five years old. The lack of specific information had a lot to do with the state of the remains when they were discovered. A body in the elements doesn't fare well, and UF526 had been undetected for many years. Scavengers will pick apart a body within hours, and what isn't consumed at the time will be carried off by rodents or washed away by the elements.

There was some damage to UF526's skull, but luckily all the facial bones were intact. Sometimes, entire portions of the face can be missing, and then it becomes a judgment call as to whether an approximation can even be attempted. If one side of the face is undamaged, it's possible to copy it and "flip" it to represent the missing half. This isn't a perfect process since faces aren't symmetrical, but it can still be worth a try.

The best way to preserve evidence is to avoid disturbing it in the first place, so that's why all facial approximations in the FBI are sculpted on 3D-printed resin replicas. I only take the evidentiary skull out to refer to it while I work; otherwise, it stays in the packaging it arrived in.

The anthropologists create a CT scan of the skull as part of their examination and forward that data to the Model Unit. The FBI has several industrial-sized 3D printers that create an exact replica by building layer upon layer out of liquid resin. Because of the amount of data required to preserve the nuances of the skull, the printing process can take up to twenty-four hours. Once the resin replica is finished, the anthropologist transfers custody of the evidentiary skull to me, and I'm ready to begin work.

After I read the anthropology report, I pick up the skull and just *look*. I take my time, and examine the skull from all angles, thinking about what the anthropologist outlined in the report and just seeing what I notice on my own. Maybe one cheek is more pronounced than the other, or the chin is noticeably pointed, or the left eye looks higher than the right. This is where the collaboration between artist and anthropologist really comes into play; we are looking at the same skull but processing that information differently. The anthropologist measures and compares angles and distances, while I picture shapes, skin folds, and flesh.

After working on so many skulls, I know the average tissue depths by heart, but I created a poster version of the chart to keep on the wall near my desk, just in case. It also shows the full range of tissue depths, so if I'm not sure whether an area is within an anatomically possible range, I can check the chart to make sure.

My sculpting room at the FBI was nothing fancy and looked like every other lab suite with fluorescent lights, metal shelving, and industrial-sized exam tables. Like most sculptors, I have a range of different tools but rely most often on the same few trusty workhorses. My favorites are the ones I've cobbled together by cutting the end of one and attaching it to another, like one that gives me a wire loop on one side and a tiny knife on the other. I also use ordinary household items, like a dry toothbrush for blending clay together, or a metal spatula to smooth large areas, like the scalp and forehead.

Before I can begin sculpting, I need to attach the mandible to the cranium of the replica skull. In life it's connected with ligaments and muscles; in death it's done with hot glue. People tend to think of skeletons as being complete and intact. Even a childhood cartoon is enough to put that image in your head forever. But, of course, bones are held in place by cartilage. When that has deteriorated and the skeleton is disarticulated (in pieces), the parts can go anywhere. That's why we will sometimes only receive a cranium for approximation. At some point, the mandible became separated from the skull, lost to the elements or scavengers.

Chris and I did a number of cases with missing mandibles, and with success too. With these, we are really at a disadvantage, because literally half the face is missing. There is no way to know if a person had a huge jutting chin, whether it was small and receding, pointed or square. The only thing we can do in those situations is to follow the artistic tenets of facial proportion and make the bottom half of the face fit with the top. It's no guarantee, but it's the best we can do in the situation.

I turned UF526's skull upside down and added small bits of cotton padding between the cranium and mandible to simulate the synovial fluid that lubricates the joint. Without that cushioning, the jaw won't fit like it did in life. Once the mandible is in place and I'm satisfied that the teeth fit together properly, I secure the replica to a sculpting stand, adjusting until it is level from front to back, and side to side, looking back squarely at me. Tissue-depth markers (I use Q-tips or coffee stirrers) come next and are applied with hot glue in their corresponding areas: point of the chin, cheekbones, brow ridges, and so on.

I usually start each sculpture by placing the eyes. There is always a bit of trial and error with this step, because the eyes need to be appropriately set in three dimensions. I fill the orbits with clay, leaving about a half-inch of space from the forward edge so I have room to make adjustments. I rub my finger along the inside of the eye orbit, feeling around for a tiny bump called the malar tubercle. This is where the outer eye ligament attaches, so the prosthetic eye needs to be about three millimeters away to allow for the thickness of the tissue.

The average human eyeball is twenty-five millimeters in diameter, so that's the size of the prosthetic I typically use. However, UF526's orbits were very large compared to the rest of her face, so I mulled over the possibility of going just a bit bigger, up to twenty-six millimeters. When I first started creating facial approximations, I never would have considered to make this seemingly minor change. Over the years, I've noticed that larger orbits tend to result in larger, more expressive eyes, just as smaller orbits result in smaller, more deeply set eyes. But owing to Jane's small stature, I decided to stick with the average.

To set the eye's depth, I turn the skull to the side and measure sixteen millimeters from the deepest edge of the orbit forward. This is where the back edge of the cornea should just touch. Most people don't realize this, but there are pockets of fat behind our eyeballs, and the amount decreases as we age. That's why people in their eighties or nineties tend to have more sunken eyes, because the fat padding has atrophied over time.

For the bottom lid, I place a thin strip of clay against the outer corner of the eye, curving it toward the lacrimal bone, a small, fingernail-sized area on the inside of the eye socket. I add the upper lid in the same way, starting at the inner corner of the eye and aiming back toward the malar tubercle. I add smaller bits of clay around the lids to keep them from moving, and then I place a layer of clay around the entire orbit. This mimics the orbicularis oculi, the muscle that encircles the eye. I don't add any more detail to the eyes, preferring to develop the whole face as a "rough draft" first.

From here, I roll out a layer of clay and apply it to the frontal bone (forehead). Then I go to the sides of the skull, adding clay behind the orbits to simulate the temporalis muscle. I work my way down the face to the sides of the jaw and form a wedge of clay about eighteen millimeters thick. This is where the masseter muscle, which runs from the sides and bottom edge of the zygomatic (cheek) bone, attaches to the mandible's bottom edge. Now, I add a smaller wedge of clay from the chin up toward the bottom teeth. There are several sets of muscles that work together with the orbicularis oris (mouth) muscle: the depressor anguli oris (which pulls the corners to the side), the depressor labii (pulls lips downward), and the mentalis (pushes bottom lip outward).

I don't sculpt these individually since they intertwine and mesh with each other to form a mass of muscle tissue. On anatomical drawings they are clearly delineated, but it would take the eye of a surgeon to differentiate them on a real cadaver. It's more important that I know the form, function, and location of each muscle, because that's what helps me give the face a more natural and realistic appearance.

The shape and thickness of the lips is really anyone's guess, because there's no structural feature on the skull that provides any clues. This is one area where I consider the age and ethnicity of the person being sculpted and use that as a guide. For instance, I'll generally make the lips of a fifty-ish White male on the thinner side and those of a twenty-year-old male a bit fuller.

I usually sculpt the mouth closed, but if there's anything unusual about the arrangement or condition of the teeth, like a missing tooth or a gap, I make sure to show it off by parting the lips. That one feature alone might be enough for someone to take notice of the sculpture and recognize the person. This is where UF526 had her most significant chance for identification: she had an extreme overbite. As in, *extremely* extreme, so much so that I asked the anthropologist to take a look and make sure it wasn't due to some postmortem change. Chris assured me that while it was unusual, it was perfectly natural.

Occasionally we'll get a toothless skull for approximation. Anthropologists can tell whether the person lost their teeth before or after death by looking at the tooth sockets. With postmortem tooth loss, the sockets will still be fully formed with the opening clearly visible. With antemortem loss, the bone will resorb, growing together and closing in on itself, resulting in a thinning of the maxilla and mandible.

Have you noticed with some older people, even when they're wearing dentures, their mouth still curves in? That's because the tooth sockets have filled in with the surrounding bony tissue. The only way to prevent this is to get dental implants, which is outlandishly expensive. I saw a skull like this once; the person had died when they were in their eighties, but they had an utterly perfect set of thirty-two pearly whites. As I marveled over it, the anthropologist said drily, "You're looking at a $100,000 mouth right there."

The nose has to be the one feature people are the most curious about. How do I know how big it is? Or whether it turns up or turns down? Or whether the person had a nose job? As it turns out, the skull gives more clues than you think. Here's one: feel under your nose. The hard part between your nostrils is a bony feature called the anterior nasal spine. This is what supports the fleshy cartilage of your nose, the part that is movable and wiggles. So, if your anterior nasal spine turns down, you will have a downward turned nose. If it points up, the tip of your nose will point up. And of course, a straight nasal spine means you'll have a straight nose.

Unfortunately, the anterior nasal spine is one of the first things rodents and scavengers go after when they find a skull, since it's fragile and can be broken easily. Depending on how much has been nibbled down, I may be able to determine the direction of the nose but will have lost crucial information about its length. In those cases, I have no choice but to depict an average nose and hope for the best.

Generally, the width of the nasal aperture (opening) is about three-fifths the overall width of the nose. If the aperture is twenty-one millimeters, I can either multiply that by five-thirds, or divide it by three and add that number (seven) to each side. Either way, the result is a total width of thirty-five millimeters. The last clue for creating the nose is a structural feature inside the aperture called the inferior nasal concha; the upper wing of the nose goes where this point begins.

By now, I've put in about eight hours of work. This is basically a "draft" of what the final sculpture will look like. It's very rough, and I've intentionally left parts of the skull exposed so I can see the thickness of the clay in areas with no tissue-depth information. Already, the sculpture is beginning to look like an individual.

The next phase is where the artistry comes in. I need to add more clay to align with the tissue-depth markers while making sure I don't lose the individuality of the face. My work slows to a crawl as I fill in the eye orbits and make light strokes into the clay to depict the eyebrows. Again, there's nothing that tells me with absolute certainty where they go, so I do my best to keep them unobtrusive. I begin the inner brow just under the edge of the orbit, angle it toward the side of the face, and then arch it slightly above the bony opening.

The skull is essentially a framework for the flesh that lies above, so I'm able to add character to the face when there are no specific guidelines to follow. The cheeks are an excellent example of this. Place your fingers beneath your nose, press firmly against your upper teeth, and then walk your fingers back on each side to feel the maxilla's shape. As you move up under your eye, you'll feel the direction change as you hit the cheekbones. The depression in that area gives me more information about how I should sculpt the cheeks.

The area of flesh on top of your cheekbones is called the malar fat pad. When the cheekbones are thick and broad on the skull, you will probably have fleshy cheeks in life, because the bone structure was formed to support a larger fat pad. Conversely, when the cheekbones are thinner and concave, the cheeks will be flatter, sunken, and less pronounced, because there isn't enough surface area to support a more substantial amount of tissue.

In short, the amount of fat and muscle on the skull is related to the size and strength of the form underneath. This holds true for the forehead, especially the glabella (or brow ridge), slightly above and between the eyes. Men tend to have much stronger brows than women, where the bone distinctively rises and dips. Typically, there is about six millimeters of tissue in the forehead area (muscle, fat, and skin combined), but when the glabellar region is very pronounced, I will build this area up more.

This Jane Doe was giving me opposing clues as far as her weight. She was relatively short, and the clothing found with her was size large, but other factors meant she could have been average weight or possibly thin. Investigators believed she was using the abandoned kiln as a makeshift home, so it's easy to assume she wouldn't have had a healthy diet. Weight can obviously vary over the years, too, so I made her look as though she had a few extra pounds on her, but nothing too drastic. Then I had her age to consider: fifty-five to eighty-five is a pretty big range. I decided to go on the lower end of the scale, reasoning it would be easier for family members to recognize a younger version of a relative, rather than envisioning a much older version.

After I work on a sculpture to about a 90 percent finish, I add the ears. There's nothing on the skull that indicates whether the person had small delicate ears or large protruding ones, so I make them fit proportionally with the rest of the face. At least I do know where to put them: they go slightly below the bony opening in the skull called the external auditory meatus, generally following the same angle as the jawline.

Hair length and style are often a guessing game, too, unless a "hair mass" sloughed off during decomposition. But it's not like the hair is ever found in a tidy pile, like a wig that has been discarded. Instead, it's usually found shredded and torn apart by scavengers, along with birds who like to use it as nesting material.

I sculpt hair in a simple, unobtrusive style, suitable for the person's age and sex. For men, that's usually a short generic haircut, and for women, a soft hairstyle brushed away from the face. It takes longer than it would by adding a wig, but it's worth it. Wigs add color information that I simply don't have, and that draws viewers' attention away from the very thing I want them to focus on: the face.

A person viewing a sculpture with brown hair and brown eyes may pass it by and not consider whether it could be their blonde, blue-eyed, sister. That's why the sculptures created at the FBI are done all in one color. Even the prosthetic eyes are monochromatic, because the whites of the glass eyes tend to stand out more than the rest of the sculpture.

When the sculpture is complete, I meet with the lead anthropologist for the case, who reviews the report and compares it to the sculpture that sits on my sculpting stand.

By now, I've put about forty hours of time in. Because the work is a collaboration, it's not uncommon for the anthropologist to recommend a few minor tweaks or have me accentuate a feature to make it more noticeable. We discuss the options back and forth until we settle on what we think is the best option.

That's exactly what I was worried about with UF526. The anthropologist approved the final sculpture, and multiple photos were sent to the investigator and medical examiner's office. The images were publicized and entered into a national database, and hopefully, someone would actually be looking for her. Investigators knew they had done all they could.

I knew that she may never be identified, and that's something that I've had to come to grips with—not just with UF526 but all the cases I've worked on. But this next step is beyond my control. A great many people have worked countless hours to return this woman to her family; the rest is up to chance.

When I first started doing facial approximations, my greatest fear was that none of them would be identified. What if I went years without an identification? Or my whole career? Worse than feeling like a failure, I'd feel that I was responsible for a victim not being identified. I would have caused more harm than good. To be honest, I didn't have much hope for UF526, but what happened next was like something right out of a movie.

FAYE AIKEN was watching TV when she saw the photos of UF526's facial approximation and listened intently to the press conference. On a hunch, she called police and told them the story of her mother who had disappeared in the late 1980s. She was somewhat of a loner, a person who preferred the outdoors and the company of her dogs over people. *Yes*, she told police, her mother was about 5'2", a bit overweight, and would have been about fifty years old when she went missing.

She remembered that her mother had been ruled out when the body in the brickyard was found, and the remains had ultimately been identified as someone else. But now that the case had been reopened, she couldn't help but think, *That might be my mother, after all.* Fingers crossed, Faye had submitted a DNA sample to police, who found it was a perfect match. UF526 had a name, and it was HELEN CAROL AIKEN.

Miles away, another daughter got remarkable news about her own mother. While one team of investigators had been pursuing the unidentified case of UF526, another team was on the missing person's case of Lily Hudson. Greta was in her backyard gardening when a detective came by to tell her that they had found her mother, alive, in Florida. Greta's missing mother, Lily Rose Hudson, had effectively been brought back to life.

I wish I knew more about what happened. Did Lily ever say why she left? Did Greta forgive her for leaving? Were they planning on meeting? I like to think that they had a happy reunion and stayed in each other's lives, but I'll never know. The most the news reports would say was that the mother left because of emotional issues, and that a reunion "might" happen in the future.

———————

Whenever there's an identification, I always study the images to see what I got "wrong," or at least what I could have done better. I want to know how closely my sculpture resembles photos of the actual person. Basically, how approximate was the approximation? For UF526, it certainly was close enough for her daughter to recognize her, but I wanted to see for myself.

Forensic artists don't always get life photos of an individual after they've been identified, because it's always up to the family whether they are released. Even when they are, the photos usually end up being a disappointment because they are too small, faded, or out of focus to study objectively. The images I received of Helen weren't much different, and I wasn't satisfied with the likeness until I looked closer.

Despite the poor image quality, it was all there: the facial proportions, the short chin, the low, fleshy cheeks. The overbite wasn't as pronounced, and that surprised me. But again, I had sculpted her with open lips to show her teeth, and in all the photos I had available, her mouth was puckered into a small, tight smile.

I was also relieved to see the variation in her weight and hairstyles over the years. Several photos showed her with shoulder-length, straight blonde hair; in others, it was short, reddish-brown, and curled. She also had light blue eyes, and her weight tended to fluctuate; sometimes she was around 180 pounds; other times, she might be a hundred pounds more. That's the thing with unidentified cases—they are moving targets.

Like most artists, I'm my own worst critic, but I couldn't help but be pleased with the outcome. I used to be afraid that my cases wouldn't be identified; now, I worry about the ones that slip through the cracks. It took many people and many years to get answers for Helen, Lily, and their daughters, and if any one of them dropped the ball, or didn't consider the importance of the work they were doing, it might never have happened at all.

12

Bogotá

Here I was again, back in Frank's office for a reason that truly felt like a punch in the gut. No, that's an understatement. More like having my insides ripped out and stomped on.

"I'm cancelling the Body Farm project." Frank said, with a satisfied grin on his face.

"What? Why?" I answered. "The second phase has been approved all the way up the chain. The money is there."

He just kept looking at me, so I thought I may have an opening to change his mind.

"We still have so much more we need to collect. When we started, most of the donors that had life photos were white males. But since our project began the university has been asking for more photos, and they've gotten them, from a wider demographic. This next trip we could probably get fifty more, we've got the process down pat now."

"How many more can you possibly need?

"Enough to round out the collection, to represent everyone. There are at least ten thousand unidentified people in the US, and over half of them are African American. Plus, we need more female samples; we only have two. Women are just as likely to be murdered, if not more so."

"No," Frank said. "What you have is plenty."

At this point, I was pleading. "Frank, please. . . . Male and female skulls aren't the same, and skulls from African Americans or Asian people aren't the same either. If we could just get more and study—"

Frank cut me short. "Your job is not to do research. Your job is to sit at your desk and do the assignments that are handed to you."

Actually, you horse's ass, the whole reason the Research Unit at the Laboratory exists is to do this exact thing: give employees the means to do their job better and share that information with other agencies. Subject-matter experts are exactly the people you should listen to when they tell you what would help them with their job. The person with the idea writes a proposal, and if the Research Unit sees value in it, the unit chief signs off and you're good to go. A research project is born, and the FBI shares what we've learned with the rest of law enforcement. That's how innovation comes about. For the first time ever, the FBI had the start of an amazing reference collection of contemporary skulls that we could share with other artists, but now it was being decimated.

So many questions, and the answers were out there. But that's how it works at the FBI. Even the chief scientist of the laboratory tried to change his mind, but Frank held firm.

I wasn't about to let him see how devastated I was; that's what he was counting on. I left his office and went to tell Wade, Kirk, and Geoff the bad news.

One day when I must have looked like I could use some cheering up, some brave soul in the Photo Unit took me aside and said there was an old case that Frank had screwed up royally. "It's all online," he whispered. "Frank said that he could tell the difference between real photos and fake ones, when he really couldn't. Anyway, just Google it, it's about a Daubert challenge. You'll see."

What on earth is a Daubert challenge, you ask? In forensic science, it's a very big deal. The gist of it is this: if you go into court professing to be an expert in a certain field and claim that you use scientific, corroborated methods for your findings, you better be able to back up that claim in court. If a person comes under a Daubert challenge, the judge can challenge your expertise and have your testimony thrown out or kept from going on record in the first place.

That's when a light went on in my brain. About a million years earlier, when I was brand new at the FBI, I remembered a day when Gary had been walking around with several photographs. He was asking artists what they thought of the images. He didn't tell anyone what he was looking for, so as not to tip his hand. It turns out that a forensic artist had created the images out of thin air, and Gary was showing them around to see if anyone could tell anything unusual about them. Was there a connection here?

I wasn't about to Google it on a work computer, because I didn't want to leave a digital trail, so I had to wait until I got home. It didn't take long to find it, a forty-three-page public spanking from a federal judge on the absolute lack of expertise of the FBI's star digital photographic expert, Franklin M. Hart Jr.

Oh, boy, I'm gonna need popcorn for this!

I printed it out, poured myself a nice glass of unoaked chardonnay, and laughed until I hiccupped.

There were some great zingers and digs at his arrogance. Referring to Frank as the government's "so-called expert," the judge pointed out the "multiple inadequacies" of his photo examination techniques and remarked that allowing him to testify would be like letting a dentist "identify the causes of glaucoma." Then came the biggest bombshell: Frank not only conceded that a digital artist might be able to produce a realistic image from scratch on the computer, he grudgingly admitted that "he would not be able to detect it if they had."

This was huge.

Frank's reputation as a digital imaging expert had just been ripped to shreds, because he said he could tell a real photograph from ones that had been created by an artist, not by using any scientifically valid methods but just by looking at it. He would never be able to testify in court again, because the defense would have a field day. This meant that his days as a forensic imaging examiner were over too.

What does the FBI do with someone who has essentially become a highly paid doorstop? They promote them. Soon after, Frank became a unit chief, where he would have to spend his days behind a desk supervising people who, unlike him, were qualified to testify as subject-matter experts.

Now, I had more insight as to why Frank despised having forensic artists in his unit. And I wondered if someone in the front office had done it just to twist the knife a little bit deeper.

I would rather look at photos of mangled bodies all day than have to see one image of child sexual assault. And normally that wasn't part of our job—the FBI has a "crimes against children" task force—but once Wade and I were asked if we could help retouch some images for a case.

We hesitated but said yes. Nobody likes working on these cases, but that's when you just try to disassociate yourself from the images, remove the emotion and get down to work. I didn't have kids, but my mental health is just as vulnerable as anyone else's. I knew it wasn't going to be pleasant and tried to steel myself for what I would be seeing and prepare for the worst.

Thankfully, the images weren't too graphic, but there was still enough context to know what had happened, or was about to. Part of our job was to "erase" the children from the images so they could be released to the public.

For instance, one image showed a man sitting on the hotel bed next to a little girl. They wanted me to remove the child and fill in the now empty area of bedspread and carpet. They were trying to figure out which hotel this was based on the design, furnishings, and the pictures on the wall, and it needed to be sanitized before being made public. Years later, only through sheer coincidence while on a tour of the National Center for Missing and Exploited Children, did I learn that she had been recovered safely, and her abductors were arrested.

Crimes against children are especially heinous, so it's especially satisfying when the perpetrators are brought to justice. One day I was eating lunch at my desk and clicking through the gossip and news when I saw this headline: Fugitive Caught Due to Incredible Age-Progressed Image. Now, this was a tabloid, not the *New York Times*, so the headlines can be pretty over the top. Plus, I don't write them. It took a second for the images to register in my brain before I said to myself, *Well, if it isn't ol' Jeff Parrish.*

I hadn't expected much when I did the age progression of him five years earlier, but I remembered the case because he was accused of having molested a four-year-old girl. There was nothing remarkable about his looks, and there was no new information to go on—no family photos, no tips from informants, nothing. But it had worked, and it was a darn-good likeness if I say so myself.

No matter how it comes about, getting a hit is always something the front office wants to know about. They need to justify budgets and their existence just like every other manager, so it was great to be able to supply them some positive ammo, so to speak.

I made a PDF of the article and sent a link to Harry, Frank, and Mr. Bean. Adding him was a little dig, to ensure that it would be seen by upper management. That was never a concern with Gary; the moment he found out about a hit or arrest, he made sure to send it up the chain. But I had already caught Harry hiding attaboys from

me, and if he didn't let me know about them, it's a good bet he hid
them from the front office too.

One Friday afternoon, Wade and I got called into the common area,
where Harry and Frank were both standing like a couple of schoolboys
snickering over a secret.

"Hey Lisa, feel like going to Bogotá tonight?"

It didn't seem like this was anything too serious, at least not based
on their attitude. They seemed to be having an awful lot of fun at
that moment, and my radar was up. I had a weekend planned with
Lauren, and she was on the I-495 Capital Beltway at that moment.
But if something real was going on, then hell yes, I'd go to Colombia.

Harry and Frank stopped giggling long enough to pull on a straight
face and announce that an agent from the Drug Enforcement Agency
had been killed, and they wanted a composite artist there immediately.

"Oh my God! Of course I'll go. When are they saying we're leaving? Tonight?

"That's what they say," Harry piped in.

"OK, so what do I do next?"

"I don't know. You'll be getting a call."

"OK. Do you know from who? Or when?"

"Nope, don't know anything yet. They just called me," Frank said.

I looked at my phone; it was almost 3:30 PM. "Is there time for
me to go home and pack and get my passport, do you think?"

"I suppose it never occurred to you to keep your passport here at
the office?" Frank sniped.

"Of course it has. But what happens if I get a call when I'm home?
Then I'd have to come to the office. So, it's a fifty-fifty chance either
way, and we're not supposed to carry our official passports with us."
Take that, smartass.

That resulted in a dirty look from Frank; I had him there.

"Well, just go back to your desk and wait, somebody will be calling you."

I didn't have the heart to call Lauren and tell her that I'd been called out on travel. She was still in traffic, and it was too late for her to turn around. Better that she get to my house and relax; then I'd tell her and Reid what was up.

While I was waiting, I started Googling. There was nothing in the news yet—no surprise there—so I went to see what I could learn about Bogotá. I was getting an uneasy feeling. Why had they been snickering? A DEA agent had been murdered, and they thought something was funny about that? Was I being set up or something?

I didn't have time to wonder. Within minutes, my desk phone started ringing. Then my BlackBerry beeped. Then my email pinged. Anything that could ring, bing, or buzz was going off all at once.

Beep!

"Do you have a visa?"

"No, I'm sorry. I don't." I had no reason to apologize; there was never any reason for me to have one until now.

"Well, your passport should be enough until we can get a temporary visa. Don't worry about it; we'll get it worked out." *Click!*

Ring!

"If we can get you out tonight, you'll probably be back tomorrow. Can you leave from the office?"

"Sure, I've got all my drawing supplies here. But—" I winced, "my passport is at home."

"That's no problem" he said brusquely, "We can get an agent to pick it up and give it to you at the airport."

This was so surreal. An FBI agent is actually going to go to my house and pick up my passport? It just felt so very Jennifer Garner in *Alias* or something. This was my first time traveling internationally for the FBI, and I had no idea how things worked, what it was like when there was an incident like this, how many people were involved, or how it was all put together. It was a whirlwind.

"It may turn out that you'll leave first thing tomorrow, so sit tight. Somebody will let you know."

I took an opportunity to call Reid and tell him that I would be at work for a while, so to go ahead and have dinner.

"Are you OK? What's going on?"

"Well, I may have to go on travel tonight. I'm not sure. Everything is so crazy, and there's a ton of people calling me."

"Well, that stinks. Lauren walked in the door ten minutes ago."

"Yeah. I didn't have the heart to tell her when she was stuck in traffic."

"So where are you going? Can you tell me?"

"Well, I know where I'm going, but I don't know if I can tell you. I don't know who's in charge or who I'm supposed to report to, and Harry and Frank went home."

"Like they'd be any help, anyway," Reid said.

I hung up with Reid and called Harry. Maybe he had found out who my contact was by now. I called his BlackBerry, knowing there was little to no chance that he'd bother answering. He didn't. I left a short voicemail to prove I had tried. I was on my own. As it turned out, I was "wheels up" the next morning, leaving Ronald Reagan Washington National Airport at 6:00 AM. I still had no idea who my contact was, or who would be meeting me at the airport.

When I landed in Miami, I struck up a conversation with a young woman while I was getting a snack, and it just so happened that she was one of the intel analysts being sent to Bogotá from headquarters. She had been fully briefed by her supervisors and had been on international deployments before, so she went over the logistics of how things worked and what I might be able to expect. Our connecting flight kept getting delayed, so we were standing at the gate waiting for another update. A few minutes later, a man came up and introduced himself as the unit chief from headquarters who would be in charge of the FBI team while in Colombia.

"How did you know who we were?" one of us asked.

"Only people from the FBI are still using BlackBerries."

Too true. Everyone else in the intelligence and law enforcement world was probably on their second version of a smartphone, but it seemed the FBI was always behind the curve, technology-wise at least. JULIAN was the type of unit chief every FBI employee wishes they had. He was cool, calm, collected, and exuded confidence. He was open and friendly, and talked to us like regular people, not as underlings or something that was on the bottom of his shoe. Plus, he was absolutely hilarious. We never lost sight of why we were there, but he saw humor in the mishaps or mix-ups that inevitably will occur, and they didn't seem to rattle him in the least.

By the time we got checked into the hotel in Bogotá, I had been awake close to twenty-four hours, and everyone else was probably in the same boat. We were all set to meet outside the hotel at 7:00 AM. We'd be working at the embassy (*Don't think about all the terrible things that have happened in other embassies!* I told myself), and we'd be taken to and from our hotel by way of armored van.

The next morning at the embassy gates we were met by at least four armed guards who did a thorough check of our credentials and the van, complete with sniffing dogs and mirrors underneath the chassis. We all assembled in the conference room where there were easily fifty people, if not more: agents from the DEA and FBI, Colombian police officers, and a bevy of stern-faced men decked out in military-grade vests and guns. I had never seen anything like this before and was in awe. You could feel the adrenaline in the air, the mission, the purpose. Everybody was there for one reason: to get the guys who killed one of their own.

Terry Watson had been assigned to the DEA's Cartagena office and was deployed to Bogotá, where he was killed during a so-called "millionaire ride." An unwitting victim gets into a taxi, whose driver is part of a gang that kidnaps passengers and then stops at multiple ATMs, forcing them to empty their bank account. Typically, the victim is beaten into submission, but Terry fought back. He was stabbed repeatedly in the backseat and was able to get out of the taxi before collapsing.

In something as serious as the murder of a US official, everyone who might possibly have anything to bring to the table was brought in. Better to have someone on-site with a skill set that turned out not to be necessary than to need a skill that nobody on the team possessed.

I was sent to do composite sketches with any potential witnesses, and I damn sure didn't want to let anyone down. But I was ready. A room had already been set aside for me, up near the guard desk at the entrance to the embassy. I settled myself in and did a little rearranging of the chairs and table to make it easier for me to talk to the witnesses. I did some warm-up drawings while I was waiting, and every so often went back to the FBI space to check on when they'd be arriving.

As it turned out, the team already had one of the suspects in their sights. Video had been collected from the surrounding buildings and examined overnight, and officers and agents were out in the field tracking him down.

With that, the legat (legal attaché) told me that it looked like they wouldn't need me for a composite sketch, at least not that day. "Go back to the hotel, relax, watch some TV, and we'll come get you if we need you."

When a senior FBI agent tells you what to do, you don't question it. But I didn't want to sit around in my room twiddling my thumbs either.

"Um, do I have to?" I asked. "I'd rather stay here and help out, if that's OK."

"Oh, OK. Sure thing." he said. He looked around the office. Then he said, "Why don't you go meet up with the intel analysts and see if there's anything they need."

From that point on, I was just as busy as everyone else. I wasn't doing anything remotely related to forensic art, but I didn't care. I was right in the middle of it, seeing firsthand all the work that goes on in a massive investigation like this. I was in the command room with the intel analysts doing the grunt work so they could spend their time on the important stuff.

The analysts would write their findings in magic marker on large sheets of paper and tape them to the wall, so at any point the agents could come in and get an overview of what information had been collected. I hate to refer to TV shows for something as serious as this, but the walls looked like what you see in most every police procedural. Photos of the current suspects with their names and aliases, rough organizational trees connecting one suspect to another, maps of neighborhoods with pins sticking to certain streets, lists of where each team was at the moment. It wasn't fancy, but it worked. The doorway was filled with a constant stream of agents, hands on hips, examining the walls and then nodding and striding off.

As more and more information came in, lines of text would be scratched out and new information would be added. Soon, the sheets would run out of room or be too messy to decipher. Normally, that's when one of the analysts would grab a new sheet of paper and redo all the current information to make a cleaner version. But that's something that I could do instead, so I'd transcribe everything and tape the new version to the wall. Before too long the sheets would get filled up and the process would start all over again.

The FBI work area within the embassy consisted of several offices on different floors, but our BlackBerries didn't reliably work in all areas of the building. Often, you'd have to stand in a certain corner of a certain room pressed against the window to get a signal. It was a hive of activity, with people literally running down the hall or flying up a set of stairs instead of waiting for the elevator. When an analyst couldn't reach someone they needed to talk to, it was my job to run upstairs and track them down, relaying messages back and forth because nobody was sitting at their regular desk when the phone rang. Even my much-despised background of data processing came in handy.

"You know Excel? Great, can you add this new section, make fifteen copies, then put it all into three-ring binders?"

"Hey, Lisa, pages sixteen to twenty-five need to be redone, but all the books have already been assembled. Can you reprint and insert the new pages, destroy the old ones, and bring them to the conference room in an hour?"

The only thing remotely related to graphics that I did was creating or making changes to PowerPoint presentations. I had never been so busy in my life, but the hours flew by. Twelve-hour days went by in a blink, and when we got back to the hotel, we'd all go to one of the restaurants across the street, have dinner, and then we'd do it all again the next day.

When FBI personnel deploy to a massive operation like this, their supervisor is kept informed of what's going on by the higher-ups. There are daily briefings and email chains copying everybody, so that way the person on travel can do their job. Every update is distributed from the top down, and everybody stays on the same page.

But even now, two thousand miles away, I couldn't get away from Frank, who pinged my BlackBerry several times a day with "What are you doing? Why are you still there?" Each time I had to stop what I was working on, find a corner where I could get a better signal, and try to explain what I was doing without saying anything classified. The analysts and agents noticed and got irritated, saying, "What's wrong with your boss? Doesn't he know you're busy?"

By the third day, Julian, the leader of the FBI team, had had enough: "Who is your section chief?"

Oh boy, he was going to call Mr. Bean and make Frank stop! And he did. I was standing behind him while he made the call, and

I wanted to cheer. Finally, someone appreciates the work I'm doing, and they were standing up for me, to boot.

But even that didn't work. The next day I was talking to the legat when my phone dinged. I looked at it and sighed. That tore it. He took the BlackBerry out of my hand and typed out a lengthy paragraph with exactly what I was doing, in a clipped managerial tone that finally let Frank know he had pissed off the wrong person.

Every so often I would have some time where there wasn't much for me to do, so I'd sit in the hallway and doodle on my sketchpad. Photos of Terry Watson were posted all throughout FBI offices, and one day I started sketching him. I couldn't take any of the pictures down because somebody would notice, so I sat across from the largest one to get the best view and drew. I didn't want anyone to see, because I was just practicing and trying keep my drawing hand loosened up.

To be honest, I hadn't ever actually done a portrait. Sure, I was drawing faces in composites, but the "likeness" was in the witness's head, it wasn't in front of me to copy. Getting a likeness of a person in a portrait is difficult. All the features can be drawn correctly, but if any one of them is a smidge too high or low, too narrow or wide, it won't look right. As John Singer Sargent, one of the most renowned artists of his time put it, "A portrait is a painting with something wrong with the mouth."

I didn't want anybody to see what would probably end up getting scribbled over in frustration. But there was another reason, one that had followed me for as many years as I can remember. While I inherited a certain amount of artistic skill from my mom, I also inherited something else: insecurity, and the inability to immerse myself in the joy of art for art's sake.

Creating something for myself, something that didn't have a deadline or purpose? Something that was done just for *me?* That's where the hard part was. For all the years I had worked at Hopkins and even now at the FBI, I still didn't feel like I was an artist. There was always an adjective before it.

What was supposed to have been an overnight trip stretched into more than a week. The legat still wanted to keep me around just in case something came up, and I was more than fine with that. I was always busy, and part of something important.

One day at lunch, the subject of vaccinations came up at the other end of the table. I hadn't been paying attention, but my ears perked up.

"We were supposed to be vaccinated before coming here?" I asked.

Somebody cleared their throat. "Well, yeah. Of course."

"You mean you weren't?" another voice asked.

"No," I said, still not getting it. "But there wouldn't have been time anyway, right?"

"Well, maybe not. But you should have at least known before you agreed to go. Anyone who could be tapped for international travel has to have a basic set of vaccinations."

OK, *now* I get it. I wasn't supposed to be here. That's why Harry and Frank were snickering. The artist who actually had that set of vaccinations was Harry. He should have gone. But of course, wouldn't it be a whole lot more fun if I were sent instead?

Despite my attempts to hide the drawing of Terry, someone must have seen me in the hall sketching. The legat came up to me with an idea. "How about you finish that drawing. Can you get it done today? I'd like to present it to the DEA at this afternoon's meeting."

Thankfully, it was close to being done, and the fact that I hadn't torn it up by now meant I felt okay about it. Not great by any means, but okay. There's a style of drawing that I always wished I had, where the work looks effortless, alive, and there's a confidence in the looseness of the lines. This wasn't it. Then again, the in-fighting between the left and right sides of my brain was still hard at work.

There are plenty of artists I admire who draw with a certain technicality, so why couldn't I let myself accept that the style I have is part of me and go with it? It's something I've dealt with much longer than I like to admit. Whenever I tried to draw more loosely, I'd get a panicky feeling in my chest, like *You're drawing outside the lines!* and I'd revert to my tighter, more precise style.

Well, I couldn't think about all that now. The sketch had become an assignment, and that's when I go right into work mode. Suggestions were made: "Can you add in the DEA shield, and this other picture of Terry to the bottom? And a flag, somewhere?"

It all became a blur; I had a couple hours until the afternoon meeting to finish and went back to the room near the guard station where I was originally going to do composites.

Finally, I handed the finished drawing to the legat with a sigh of relief. I thought the legat would be presenting it to the DEA at the end of the meeting. Instead, I heard him say my name, and would I please come up to the front and hold up the drawing? First there was silence, and it felt like the air had been sucked out of the room. These people loved Terry Watson. Even those who had never met him loved him. He was their brother-in-arms, the embodiment of everything they held important: service, duty, allegiance to each other and the mission. I'm not trying to be maudlin, but these men and women take the job *very* seriously.

I was taken aback when several DEA agents came up to me afterward with tears in their eyes, still in full tactical gear. Several shook my hand; others just gave a firm nod of their head. It was an emotional way to end the day, and quite simply, a moment in my life that I will never forget.

13

Throne of Lies

I felt like I was taking crazy pills. While one arm of the agency was doing everything in its power to bully me into dropping my complaint, the other was using me as a media tool to promote the bureau. One day, I would be accused of insubordination, threatened with termination or the loss of my clearance, the next I would be chosen to be interviewed by the *Washington Post*.

I nearly threw my computer across the room one day after seeing the FBI's YouTube channel. There was a video on how hard the bureau works to identify deceased victims, featuring—wait for it—me. How ironic and insulting can you get? See the nice lady sculpting? See how much she cares? I bet if they had a video of agents romping through a field of puppies, they would have used that instead. I was tempted to write in the comments, *Help me! Someone, please, help me!* Of course, I didn't, but at least I made myself laugh about it for a moment.

Still, there was one thing that I was thoroughly happy about: Dr. Bunsen retired. I think the whole Laboratory cheered at that, because he wasn't exactly a popular person. When SAMUEL NORTON was named the director, I allowed myself to be hopeful again. Maybe things would change, since Dr. Bunsen had been the one keeping me in the hell of the Photo Unit.

Sure enough, Mr. Norton called me into his office with some great news. "How would you like to go to the Science Unit?"

Are you kidding me? I'd love it! Thank you, yes! A million times yes!

But there was a condition. I needed to drop the EEO.

Well, shit. I wanted nothing more than to be done with the whole mess, especially because I had never wanted to start it in the first place. But this seemed fishy. What did one thing have to do with the other? The party line was that there's no interference in the EEO process, and this sure seemed like interference to me. I decided to address the elephant in the room.

"What about the money?" I asked. "Will the FBI reimburse me for everything I've had to spend on lawyers?" At this point Reid and I were more than $30,000 in debt, money that never would have been spent if Bunsen had done the right—and legal—thing. If he had kept his word on my mediation agreement, I wouldn't be in this predicament.

"Well, I don't know if I can do anything about that," he said. "Maybe I could talk to the FBI lawyer . . ." His voice trailing off.

I was halfway considering it, just cutting my losses and moving on. The way the FBI kept throwing motions at my lawyer and drowning me in paperwork, Reid and I could end up owing two or three times what we already did. But why did they make me go through this whole nightmare in the first place?

Reid and I talked it over, and he had the same reaction I did. *Why would Norton's word be any better than Bunsen's?*

In the midst of the EEO proceedings, Harry and Frank continued looking for ways to harass me. One of their favorites was to play a game called "Let's screw around with Lisa's casework and try to make her head explode." They both knew I took my job seriously and would have rather cut off a limb than miss a deadline, so that's another way they could get their digs in. Another game they would play was "I can't do it now; I'll do it tomorrow."

The case I was working on was essentially a sting operation where a task force was trying to bring down a human trafficking operation and needed thirty fake driver's licenses to use as bait. Nowadays, faces can be created with artificial intelligence, but in 2012 it still had to be done the old-fashioned way, by an artist with Photoshop.

The agents would take care of making the false licenses. My job was to create thirty people that didn't really exist. I know that the bureau has been accused of not taking the protection of personal information seriously, but I can tell you here they weren't about to stomp over civil liberties and use real photos. A cynic might say that the bureau was just afraid of getting sued, but no matter how it shakes out, the agent took pains to ensure that everything was on the up and up.

I needed to sort through hundreds of arrest photos and make fake people out of them. They had to be all different ages and races, and to keep the bad guys from suspecting anything, no feature could be used more than once, not even ears, hair, or the type of shirt the person was wearing. If any one of the suspects had noticed two photos with a person wearing the same glasses, that would blow the whole operation, and possibly even the cover of any undercover agents who were involved.

I had two weeks to create all thirty, and at a pace of three or four images a day, I could pull it off. Everyone else in the unit was as busy as I was with their own cases, so the work couldn't be split up among us. I thought it was most reasonable to send the images to the agent in batches; that way he could assure the rest of the task force that everything was on track. Also, I wanted to make sure that what I was sending him was acceptable. In my mind, there was no sense in sending him all thirty at the end of the month for him to tell me that the background wasn't right or something.

Even though a federal judge had made it abundantly clear to the
world that Frank was incapable of detecting digital photo manipulation, he still insisted that he check all my work, which of course, was
digital photo manipulation. But he was always too busy.

"I'm too busy right now. I'll do it after lunch," Frank said.

Except when Frank got back from lunch Harry wasn't around, and
of course Frank didn't want to check them until Harry was there. This
went back and forth for days, when lo and behold both of them were
out of the office. At a retirement party at headquarters.

Now I had to wait until the frat boys got back from Washington,
if they even came back at all. It's not uncommon for retirement parties
to end up as happy hours, especially on a Friday. They finally breezed
in around 3:00 PM, spent a grand total of fifteen seconds looking over
my shoulder, scribbled their initials, and left. I got the photos out to
the agent, and the thumbs-up to keep going.

I wasn't going to give them the satisfaction of letting them know
I was pissed off, but it was just one more thing that went into my
"ammo" file. I had saved every single email where they were playing
"tag" with my casework, or purposely delaying assigning it to me.

While I was waiting for my case to be assigned to an administrative
judge, I would entertain myself by reading articles about how to prevent workplace bullying. Every one gave the same advice, and none
of it was helpful.

*Stand up to them! Let them know you won't take it! Once they realize
you won't tolerate their behavior they'll respect you and treat you better.*

One article wrote that winning an EEO case would be especially challenging because it was nearly impossible to gather concrete
evidence.

Most supervisors are too intelligent and well trained to put discriminatory statements in writing.

Yay! Mine weren't that smart—that was for sure. When I realized things were going seriously sideways in 2010, I started saving everything. Every email with Harry or Frank's name on it, no matter how innocuous, I saved. Who knew whether I might need it later? In the security field it's drilled into our heads that one little puzzle piece might seem insignificant, but put 'em all together and you just might have incontrovertible evidence of wrongdoing.

I had done the same thing all through the Brent debacle. I made PDFs of everything: the emails that went back and forth, every shred of documentation to prove what I had said or done was true. That's the upside to being a perfectionist with just a dash of obsessive-compulsive behavior thrown in.

I didn't stop with emails either. Harry had created a database where he would grade us on the cases we had just finished, like schoolkids. As if all the hits, successful closed cases, and commendation letters weren't enough.

That's when I discovered that he had changed my marks. I had never been graded anything less than excellent, but now they were different—I had a slew of unsatisfactory and average marks. *That sonofabitch. He's going to try to use this against me in the EEO to show what an abysmal worker I was.*

But he had another thing coming. I had already taken screenshots and created PDFs of every work order he had ever assigned me. Each page was timestamped, so I would be able to prove to the administrative judge that this was an act of retaliation. Plus, an FBI employee was falsifying official FBI records.

I knew I could prove my case once I got my hearing. I had solid, irrefutable evidence, and I used my background in demonstrative evidence to make it crystal clear for the judge, or anyone on the outside looking in, to understand what had been going on.

I created interactive PDF presentations, highlighting each lie in management's sworn statement, then linking it to each document. When Harry said he never delayed casework or falsified records, I linked to the email chain and database to prove he had done exactly that. When Frank declared under oath that I was insubordinate and impossible to manage, I linked directly to emails from him, Dr. Bunsen, Mr. Bean, and outside agencies praising me for my professionalism and outstanding performance.

I had everything: every email, nasty instant message, even audio files of the insane voicemails Harry would leave harassing me after hours.

One, in particular, was a doozy. Desperately needing to get away from the stress and madness at work, Reid and I decided to go to Vegas, the best place in the world to blow off steam. And it was our tenth anniversary, so we decided that it would be hilarious to renew our vows while we were there. With an Elvis impersonator, of course.

My BlackBerry was locked away in the safe and I would check it every night. I wasn't obligated to, since I wasn't an on-call employee— what's more, I was on vacation. But I did it just in case something major came up.

I didn't tell Reid this during the trip, because he would have been livid, but Harry left me a voicemail chewing me out, accusing me of being AWOL. He had actually deleted my leave request himself and didn't count on the fact that I had kept a copy of it to throw in his face when I got back.

Besides the constant harassment and gaslighting, there's the character assassination. Management spreads the word that you are toxic, and your coworkers are "strongly advised" that they better not be seen talking with you. Not at the watercooler, not in the hallway, not even walking across Hogan's Alley to go to one of the incessant town hall meetings. Everyone would walk together in groups, chatting and laughing along the way, but I stayed on the perimeter. I'd catch someone's eye, and they'd look away quickly like *Please don't catch up with me.*

And I wouldn't, because I didn't want to put them in that position. I was already well acquainted with threats and reprisal and knew they were real, and didn't want my friends to be collateral damage.

Management is hoping that the pressure and isolation from their coworkers will wear the employee down and they'll decide to quit. This has the added benefit of making the EEO complaint go away, because it's an administrative process. Why keep fighting an uphill battle in the name of justice when you don't even work there anymore? This is what's called "compelling termination." It's illegal, so naturally the FBI has perfected the technique.

It's a horrible, demeaning, exhausting amount of pressure to be put on a person, and it might have worked on me, if I was in any other type of job. But being a forensic sculptor at the FBI is kind of like being Liam Neeson, in that "I have a very particular set of skills."

If there was any place else in the world I could have possibly gone, I might have considered it. The CIA is amazing, and I'd be really proud to work there, but it's not as if they had any openings, and who's to say they'd hire me anyway? Positions there were just as highly prized as they were at the bureau. Besides, the CIA only does international cases, so I wouldn't get any facial approximations other than the occasional dead terrorist.

I could give up forensics altogether, leave the FBI, and go back to regular ol' graphics, but I wouldn't let myself consider it. I loved it too much. I had worked all my life to get here. Forensics was where I wanted to be. Furthermore, I was good at it. In fact, I was damn good. Why should I have to be the one to leave?

People tend to think it's difficult to fire a government employee, especially one who doesn't deserve it. But it's really pretty easy when you have a management chain that is hellbent on making it happen and has no qualms about lying under oath along the way.

At the FBI there are two ways to go about it: the first is the preferred method, because it's pretty foolproof. No other divisions are involved, so an unscrupulous supervisor doesn't have to worry that some do-gooder in another part of the Bureau will thwart their plans by following FBI regulations.

Here's how easy it is: First, the supervisor marks the person down on their yearly performance appraisal. This usually comes as a complete surprise to the employee and should serve as a warning that management is up to no good. Next, the supervisor meets with the employee to discuss their failing marks. There's no written record of the conversation for the employee, so the supervisor can claim anything.

Then management helpfully places the employee under a performance improvement plan (PIP), the outcome of which is preordained. The requirements are impossible to meet—they're either hyperspecific or extremely vague—and management has no intention of helping the employee improve. When the employee fails, they will be warned that they could be fired for bad performance.

This mortifies the employee, because they did everything that management asked and it still wasn't good enough. They know that to be sacked from the FBI means losing their clearance, which makes them damaged goods in the security world. This is when management kindly offers them an out: just quit. Tell people that "you need to spend more time with family," say you got a better job offer, whatever. Quit before we bring the hammer down, and nobody needs to know. It all goes away, and you can keep your security clearance and start fresh somewhere else.

The added benefit for the FBI is heading off a potential lawsuit, since the employee quit "of their own volition." Even if the employee stood their ground and ended up being let go, the FBI isn't likely to worry about legal ramifications; it has plenty of lawyers.

But what if a PIP isn't enough? What if the supervisor wants blood? What if their end goal is to ruin a person's reputation, destroy their career, revoke their clearance, and destroy any possibility of ever working in the federal sector again? That's when they go for the jugular and invoke the most frightening acronym known in the federal workforce: the OPR.

OPR stands for the Office of Professional Responsibility, the division of the FBI that investigates personnel for alleged wrongdoing. It's a sword that hangs over the head of every employee, because it's often used as a ruse to get a person fired, valid or not. It's even a verb in the bureau: "Oh my God, I've just been OPR'd!"

Just like a PIP, it doesn't matter that the employee hasn't done anything wrong. But if you really want to show an employee who's the boss and make them rue the day they ever stood up to you, an OPR is the way to go.

OPRs aren't always a slam dunk, because the paperwork has to go up to headquarters where someone might do their due diligence and discover that there was no merit to the charges. That's a chance the division is willing to take, since OPRs take more than a year or two to settle. In the meantime, the supervisor gets a front-row seat to your misery. Everything you do or say is put under the microscope, questioned, and challenged as they try to add more fuel to the OPR fire. They will twist the facts, muddy the waters, and outright lie.

I had been walking on eggshells for years, doing my best to avoid anything that might give Frank ammunition to use against me. I discovered that his first attempt to start an OPR against me happened days after I filed for mediation. Frank had sent a pack of lies to the Office of Integrity and Compliance lawyer MARK TYLER under the pretense of being concerned about my website and "social media activity." But he ran up against something he probably never expected: an FBI employee who followed FBI regulations and wasn't swayed by personal vendettas.

Mark went over everything with a fine-toothed comb and wrote to Frank that he could relax, "Ms. Bailey has done quite well in not mentioning her FBI affiliation," so there's nothing to worry about. I'm sure there was some teeth gnashing on Frank's part, but it didn't stop him. Like throwing spaghetti on a wall, Frank would continually send new "concerns" to Mark, but none of them ever stuck, since, you know, I wasn't doing anything wrong.

But now there was a new FBI integrity and compliance lawyer in town. After several long conversations with Frank, she looked at the exact same information that Mark had deemed to be perfectly within FBI regulations and decided otherwise.

"You have violated FBI regulations. You are ordered to delete your website."

"OK," I wrote back. "Does this apply to everyone?"

I pointed out that several men inside and outside my unit had websites, which, unlike mine, featured their FBI status prominently. Why was I being singled out? I attached screenshots of the letters that Dr. Bunsen, Mark, and the lawyers in the Office of Integrity and Compliance had signed years before, confirming that I was allowed to operate my website. Maybe, just maybe, they would realize that what they were doing was distinctly discriminatory and sexist.

That's when the big boss, the director of the Office of Integrity and Compliance *himself* wrote back to me, incensed that I had dared to point out the obvious. And that, long story short, is how I got OPR'd.

Every so often in the FBI you'll see a security officer and the human resources unit chief walking down the hall together. When this happens, everybody's heart stops. When those two are together, you know somebody's getting walked out, and all you can do is sit there and pray as the beads of sweat pop up on your forehead that they walk past you.

Usually, they try to clear everybody out of the floor when something like that is going to happen, but sometimes there are a few people milling about. One time, I saw them coming down the hallway and was sure they were headed for me. So did a lot of other people, apparently. I would bump into someone that I hadn't seen in a while, and they'd exclaim, "Hey, you're here! I heard you had been walked out!"

I always used to wonder, *Doesn't the person know they're under investigation?* Shouldn't they have some sort of clue for what's about to happen? I was constantly worried that I would be next. But there was nothing I could do to prepare for the possibility. My back was up against a wall. The FBI lawyers were trying to bankrupt us with the EEO, while taking away any possibility of quitting and moving on.

Leaving a federal job while under OPR investigation is just as bad as being fired. You are damaged goods, untrustworthy, and certainly not to be trusted with a clearance. In security parlance, you are a "burn bag," one of those red-striped paper sacks used to hold old classified material before it's thrown into an incinerator.

If I left now, that's what I would be: classified trash.

The only thing that kept me going during the years of abuse was my casework. Never in my life have I missed a deadline, and I wasn't about to let my work performance slide. If I had to stay late, come in early, or work weekends without pay, then that's what I did.

The FBI's twisted logic used that work ethic against me. When I was deposed, the FBI lawyer asked me sarcastically, "So after these supposed episodes of your supervisor yelling at you, what did you do? Did you cry? Did you have to go to the ladies' room for half an hour to compose yourself?"

"No" I replied. "I had deadlines."

"You mean you just kept on working like nothing happened?"

"Well, no. I was upset, but I still had a job to do and field agents who were depending on me to meet their deadlines."

"Did the quality of your work suffer? Did you make lots of mistakes that had to be fixed? Did you get any complaints?"

"No, no, and no," I replied.

"Well then," the lawyer said, "how can you possibly say that you were in a hostile work environment, if you were still able to do your job exactly as you had before?"

Kids, this is the reasoning of the FBI.

One thing I couldn't understand was why the FBI was going to such lengths to save the butts of two men who were clearly thumbing their noses at FBI regulations and discrimination law while spending thousands of dollars and hundreds of man hours in the process.

Both were easily replaceable, as paper-pushers go. As a first-line supervisor, Harry was the lowest form of managerial life. Yes, Frank was higher up as a unit chief, but then again, he wasn't an agent (which counts, believe me), and more to the point, he was no longer a qualified examiner. The whole situation dumbfounded me. I just couldn't understand why the FBI was going to so much trouble to get rid of me and save them.

And then it occurred to me: *It was no trouble at all.* It was ingrained in the culture, and all the rules and actors were in place. The FBI does everything by procedure, and they had the process down pat. It had been perfected and polished over the years, honed, a finely tuned reprisal machine, set to autopilot.

They weren't coming after me, Lisa, a human being and member of the FBI family. They were coming after complaint number BR549, something that had the potential to tarnish the FBI's impossibly perfect reputation where supposedly nobody ever does anything wrong, ever.

It wasn't personal. It was just business. They might as well have had the slogan painted on the front door of headquarters: REPRISAL: IT'S WHAT WE DO!

How did I keep my sanity and my sense of humor during the unrelenting pressure? Years of being threatened, diminished, mocked, insulted, gossiped about, cyberstalked? For a time, I didn't. I may have joked about my OCD-ness and perfectionism, but I've dealt with varying levels of diagnosed anxiety my whole life. Add in a great big dose of gaslighting and abuse, and you've got a recipe for disaster. At times, I truly felt like I was close to having a mental breakdown, and on June 13, 2013, it very nearly happened.

Have you ever heard of a derecho? I hadn't, until one hit Fredericksburg, Virginia, in the summer of 2012. Reid and I were home when it happened, and it was truly terrifying. A line of thunderstorms six hundred miles long with winds up to ninety miles an hour swept from Indiana to Virginia, coming on as quickly as a tornado. It killed twenty-two people, caused $3 billion in damage, and forced millions of people to sweat through 96-degree heat while the power was out for almost a week.

These events were nothing to mess with. The following year when another derecho was predicted to be coming in our direction, the front office strongly advised employees to put in a leave request for the following day. I submitted mine immediately. I reminded Harry that afternoon; these things can kill people, so please approve my leave request. I was anxious, because Harry was actively looking for reasons to write me up, even for something as stupid as rubber-stamping leave requests.

"I'll get to it," he answered.

The morning of the incoming derecho I asked him again. I stood in his doorway waiting, and he said angrily, "I told you I'd get to it!"

An hour later, when it *still* wasn't approved, I left voicemails on his desk phone and BlackBerry, because he wasn't in his office. Still nothing. I knew he was at work—he had approved Wade's leave request within five minutes. I kept calling every fifteen minutes or so, but he never answered. Around lunch, the winds started kicking up, and the unit was emptying out. I was frantically knocking on doors, trying to find Harry. I was entering full-on panic mode. At this point, he had either gone home or was under a desk hiding from me. *Which was worse?* I thought. *Risking life and limb driving through hurricane-strength winds, or getting OPR'd again?* I chose life.

The next morning, Harry barged into the office and headed straight for me. "You shouldn't have left yesterday! Your leave request wasn't approved. . . . You should have tried to find me. . . . You should have called me. . . . You should have reminded me. . . . You can't leave until I say you can . . . " and on and on until I thought I would scream.

I tried to get away, because I couldn't tolerate being near him, but he kept following me around the room, yammering, ignoring me when I said, "Please get away from me! I put in my leave request twenty-four hours in advance, but you always put off signing it. I *did* try to find you, but I couldn't. I *did* go to your office, but you weren't there. I *did* call you, but you never answered."

This is the sort of thing that sounds crazy when you tried to explain it to somebody, because it *was* crazy. And I seriously thought I might crack. Finally, I ran out the door to another supervisor's office and begged, "Could you please make Harry leave me alone? He won't stop yelling and following me around. I try to get away from him, but he keeps coming after me!"

The supervisor's mouth was still hanging open when Harry came up behind me and started right back in again. And at that point I freaked. I just took off, left the office, and ran outside to pull myself together. I couldn't take it anymore. It was insanity.

When I got back to my desk, people steered clear. Maybe it was because they heard that I had lost it, or maybe it was my "do not mess with me" demeanor. I felt like the velociraptor in *Jurassic Park*.

If anyone so much as looks at me sideways, I swear I will rip out their throat and dissolve their face with acid.

14

Out of the Woods

A miracle occurred in the summer of 2014. A supervisory position opened in the Graphic Unit, and DARLA, the unit chief, was looking to hire a replacement. Unfortunately for her, the front office rewarded Harry with the spot. Wade would be transferred along with Harry, who would now supervise a total of fifteen artists. I felt bad for Wade—he loved doing facial approximations, and it was being taken away from him—but Darla was getting what she deserved. After all, she sang Harry's praises in her sworn statement during the EEO investigation. As for me? I was being sent to the Science Unit.

Walking into that door reminded me of the first time I saw *The Wizard of Oz* on a color TV. I entered a bright, shiny land full of forensic examiners and scientific professionals who smiled and said hello to me in the hallway, and nobody yelled, ever.

But I was nervous. I was still in the middle of the EEO and OPR investigations, and I felt like this might be some kind of a setup. It was too good to be true. My entire job would be facial approximation and postmortem imaging. I would have a room to myself and sculpt all day, every day.

I would report directly to the unit chief, MELANIE, and worried what she must think of me. Certainly, she had heard all the rumors, and I knew Frank would have been unscrupulous enough to tell her horror stories about me. It all came out in the open when the unit had a trip planned to a minor-league baseball game. I was brand-new to the unit and wanted to go but couldn't, because it fell on the same day that I was being deposed for the OPR.

I told Melanie, "I know people have said terrible things about me, but it's not true, I promise. Please keep an open mind and let me prove myself to you."

And she did, which I will forever be thankful for. I was able to start with a fresh slate and tried to push the EEO and OPR out of my mind. I inherited Wade's open cases, so my workload now doubled, and I had to play catch-up. But I certainly wasn't complaining. Plus, I got to do work that never would have been allowed under the old regime.

It was a project that I desperately wanted to do: the National Museum of Health and Medicine, outside Washington, asked the FBI whether it could help put a face to an anonymous skull from the Civil War, which belonged to an unknown African American soldier who fought in the Fifty-Fourth Massachusetts regiment. The skull had been found in 1876 on Morris Island, South Carolina, near the site of the battle of Fort Wagner. Remains of a one-inch iron projectile found in the skull were consistent with those fired from a Confederate howitzer.

It would require permission from the front office, and thankfully, they said yes. The condition was I had to work it in between my actual casework. That was fine by me. I told Melanie that I would do it at home on my own time if I had to.

Normally, I would have the actual skull to work from, but this was a precious item. There couldn't be any chance that any damage might come to it, and I didn't want the pressure of being responsible for it anyway. The museum had a CT scan of the skull, so the data file was sent to us. Kirk fired up the 3D printer, and several days later I had the resin copy.

But I really needed another copy so I could keep this one to refer to. Costs wouldn't allow a second resin print, so I went old-school and created my own using silicone for the mold and plaster for the skull copy. This was my first introduction to what I'd envisioned my sculpting life might be like in retirement. At work, I'd been a problem solver, and it was easy to get the creative juices going when working within the confines of a problem. But increasingly, I looked forward to opportunities to break out of the restrictions that are inherent in facial approximation.

I'm embarrassed to admit how long it took. It was over a year, and although I could blame it on the fact that I was working on it bit by bit, putting it aside as soon as a new case came in, I knew the real reason. Fear. Yellow, stinking fear. I was afraid I wouldn't do him justice. I was afraid the museum wouldn't like it. I was afraid I wasn't adding enough detail. I was afraid of adding too much. Finally, I had to let it go. I wish I could have done it better, but for the life of me, I don't know what better would look like.

One of the cases that took me away from the Civil War sculpture was unique in that we were asked to do a facial approximation from the skull, but without the skull. It was a cold case from 1995, and the requesting agency explained that somewhere along the way the skull had been lost, cremated, or buried. Nobody knew exactly what happened to it, but they didn't want to give up trying to identify the young man.

What they did have were two faded Polaroids of the skull, so the question was, could we do a 2D approximation from that? The photos hadn't been taken with a ruler for scale, so figuring out tissue depths would be an issue. In one photo, the skull was sort of tipped back, as though it were looking up, and not straight on toward the camera.

Should I draw over the skull as it was, or should I attempt to tilt it more forward in my sketch so it was straight on, facing the camera? I decided straight on was best. The second photo was a side view, so I used that to transfer the facial features and measurements into a front view and make up for the perspective distortion.

I did the sketch with Photoshop and a digital stylus on a pressure sensitive screen. It feels exactly like drawing and is much more efficient than trying to draw over a light table and tracing paper, as I had to do in the past. I did the sketch; Chris gave it the thumbs-up; and the images went out. And then, nothing. For a couple of years, if I remember right. Investigators were going to heroic lengths to identify him, and they must have spent hundreds of hours. But still, nothing.

Then an organization called the DNA Doe Project got involved. They combed through genealogy sites and found several possibilities. The sketch I had done bore a resemblance to one driver's license among the prospects, so the John Doe's DNA was compared against the DNA in the database. It turned out to be a match, and when Chris and I saw the young man's photo we couldn't help but be pleased with the resemblance. Against all the odds, a twenty-five-year-old cold case was solved.

The cases we get for facial approximation come from all over the United States, but the case of 760UFVA hit very close to home. The remains had been found in 1991 by Civil War buffs doing some exploring in Stafford, Virginia, around the I-95 highway. There's still plenty of nature around the highways in Virginia, and that's one of the things I liked about living there. Every square foot of nature hadn't been dug up and paved over; even the medians dividing the north and south lanes were natural grassy areas, some parts still densely populated with trees.

This is what I had to go on from the anthropology results for 760UFVA: a woman of Latin American descent, thirty to forty-five years old at the time of death, standing about five feet tall, and weighing between 100 and 125 pounds. The remains were entirely skeletal, so hair color and eye color were unknown. Odds would say that being of Latin American descent, I could have safely added dark hair to the sculpture, but again, that's not how it's done in the FBI. The sculpture was done like every other one I had done before, monochromatic in tone.

Normally, I only show teeth in a sculpture when there is something unusual about them, but these were perfect. She did, however, have a slightly receding chin, so it seemed like she might have the type of mouth where the teeth would show a bit, even when not smiling. Think of the actor Jon Heder, or even Taylor Swift in certain photos. There was no way to know that for sure, and Chris and I didn't want to draw attention to something that might not have been there. So I sculpted her with a very slight smile to show her teeth, but nothing so obvious that it would stand out.

When I learned that 760UFVA had been identified, it confirmed that not adding hair color was the right choice. She was an attractive young woman in full makeup, eyes rimmed with blue eyeliner and bright red lips that reminded me of Taylor Swift. And her hair wasn't brown or black but a bright strawberry blonde. My sculpture looked somewhat bland in comparison, but the resemblance was certainly there. She had been identified, and that's where I left it.

In the past I might have Googled her name to see what else I could learn about her, or see if there were any other photos for comparison, but I stopped doing that after a while. It just seemed my time was better spent looking forward.

Fast-forward twelve years to March 2019. People were stopping me in the hallway and saying, "Hey, I saw you on *Dateline* last night!"

"Really? Are you sure? I've never done anything for *Dateline*."

"I'm sure it was you. It was on near the end, like the last ten minutes. Go look it up!"

I went to my desk, pulled up the episode, and fast-forwarded to the end. There I was, sculpting away. I was already familiar with this snippet of footage, because it's the same one that had been posted on the FBI's Facebook and YouTube pages. NBC didn't have to ask permission from either me or the FBI since everything on a government website is public domain. I didn't think too much of it at the time, because it happens. Once you're online in something the government has produced, your face can show up when you're least expecting it.

I didn't watch the whole episode, because I was at work and I kept forgetting to watch it when I got home. I knew it was about a woman who had gone missing and was thought to have been killed by her boyfriend. That was sad enough for me, so I didn't make an effort to watch it. But when I finally did, it blew me away. Not just for the twists and turns of the case, but for the tenacity of one victim's brother, and the dedication of a detective who set out to solve one missing person case and ended up solving two.

Pamela Butler vanished from her Washington, DC, home in February 2009. Her mother was immediately worried; they had plans for Valentine's Day dinner, but Pam never showed up. When calls to Pam's phone went unanswered, she asked her son Derrick to go with her to Pam's house. Everything was spotless, just the way Pam normally kept things, except for the mail still sitting on the doorstep.

One thing that caught the mother's attention were the blinds in the dining room. They were the kind that you could either pull down from the top or lift from the bottom, and she knew Pam would only pull them down from the top. She was very security conscious; that way she could look out without anyone from the outside seeing her. But when the mother saw that the shade had been lifted from the bottom, she became more concerned. Something had happened to her daughter, and Pam was reported missing.

When police reviewed the security tapes, they saw both Pam and her boyfriend, José Rodriguez-Cruz, go into the apartment in the evening, but only Jose leaving the next day. He had been seen carrying bags out of the house days afterward, and explained to police that they had just broken up and he was removing his belongings. That sounds reasonable, but as any true crime aficionado knows, if there's a missing person and somebody is carrying trash bags, there's something other than trash in those bags.

But that didn't seem to be the case here. Police had been over her house with a fine-toothed comb, and there was no indication of any blood, nothing to indicate a struggle, nothing to indicate a crime had occurred at all. But where was Pam? The only answer that made sense was that José had killed her and had somehow disposed of her body without being detected.

Pam's brother was very vocal, going on TV and giving interviews over the years, unhappy with the lack of progress on his sister's case. In August 2016 the family made the difficult decision to have Pam declared legally dead. It had been seven years with absolutely no word, no activity on any of her bank accounts or credit cards, and no indication that she was alive.

Then, in February 2017, Washington, DC, cold case detective Mike Fulton came on board, eager to solve "one of the hard ones." Inheriting an unsolved homicide case worked in his favor over a missing person's case. "If we figure out who did it, we can make an arrest and at the arraignment hearing a defense attorney can't say, 'Look, Pam Butler is alive, and she's going to walk through this door.'"

José had gone on with his life after Pam's disappearance and had even gotten married. Detective Fulton went back to square one, dug into José's past, and learned more about his history of violence against women. Looking through old police reports, he found that José had been accused of an assault and attempted kidnapping of a woman in 1989. When she didn't appear for the court date, the case was dropped. That woman was actually his first wife, Marta Haydee Rodriguez-Cruz.

They had a son, Hansel, who had grown up thinking that his mother had abandoned him. Now an adult, he described to Detective Fulton a life of terror living with his father. In one of the many violent outbursts he witnessed as a child, José began threatening his stepmother with a gun, so Hansel ran to another room to hide. There he saw what looked to be a suicide note written by José saying that he was responsible for Marta's disappearance.

But that didn't make sense to Detective Fulton, who knew Marta was alive and well living in Florida. That had been confirmed in 2000 when Miami-Dade police went to her home and spoke to her after an alert in a missing person's database. The woman who answered the door had the driver's license, social security number, and all the proper identification. Marta's name was subsequently removed from the missing person database.

But Fulton was curious. He decided to try to find a photo of the woman police had contacted in Florida, and when he got it, he compared it with a picture of Marta. *It wasn't her.* When confronted, the woman who had presented herself as Marta confessed to police she was actually a cousin of José Rodriguez-Cruz. That's when Detective Fulton went to his boss's office, plopped in a chair, and said, "Dude, he was married before, and his wife is missing. What if he killed his first wife?"

On April 8, 2017, just two months after Detective Fulton took over the case, José Rodriguez-Cruz was arrested for the murder of Pam Butler. He initially claimed innocence and then broke down and confessed in the face of overwhelming circumstantial evidence. But he wanted a deal: he would plead guilty for second-degree murder in exchange for a reduced sentence of twelve years. The condition was, he had to show police where he had buried Pam. On October 6, 2017, the deal was struck. But if he misled police or did not make a legitimate effort to provide the location, the offer would be null and void.

On December 10, 2017, Washington, DC, police closed down a section of I-95 and searched the median strip where José said he had disposed of Pam's body. While Derrick was watching from an overpass, he called a local news station saying that cadaver dogs had detected remains. But because of construction on that stretch of highway over the years, her body could not be found.

Derrick and his family were deeply disappointed. All they had wanted was to give Pam a proper burial, and they were being denied that. They understood that police had done all they could, but they didn't think the plea agreement should be honored since her remains weren't found.

But it wasn't over yet. News of the search led to a revelation. Virginia police notified DC prosecutors that *another* woman's body had been found in 1991, very close to the median and only a few miles away. Was there a connection?

A DNA sample from Hansel Rodriguez was compared with the case from 1991, and on June 13, 2018, Marta Rodriguez-Cruz was positively identified. And that was the case of the facial approximation that I had done in 2006: 760UFVA.

But justice hadn't been completely served. Not yet. José could still be released from prison after serving the twelve-year sentence for Pam's murder. Two years later, on March 4, 2020, José was arrested for Marta's murder. He pled guilty, and on April 9, 2021, he was sentenced to forty years in prison.

It was eerie, thinking of driving past the area where both women had been buried. Both were near the Garrisonville exit, the same one that I took every day to work for eighteen years. And it was mind-boggling too, thinking how everything had come about. If it hadn't been for the persistence of Derrick, the brother of Pam Butler, who had gone missing in 2006, neither of the two cases could have been solved.

Work was everything I'd ever hoped it could be, but through this period my mom's health weighed heavily on me. She was in the hospital several times a year, first with a broken wrist, then a broken ankle, then unexplained bleeding, then pneumonia, then rehab and back to assisted living, where a month or so later something else would happen.

No matter how gently we spoke to her about the inevitability of death for everyone, she refused to think about end-of-life directives, much less sign a do-not-resuscitate order. Each time she came back from the hospital she was weaker than before, but even at ninety-three she was like the Energizer Bunny; somehow, she just kept on going.

The one thing she was adamant about was that she wanted to move back to Dover, Delaware, where my brothers Jeff and Ken lived. "I've loved being close to you and Lauren here, but I don't like Virginia. I want to go home." It was a request that was impossible to refuse.

When Lauren and I got a flurry of texts from Jeff in January 2018, we expected it to be about Mom. But it was about Ken. He was in the emergency room with severe head trauma; he had fallen on cement while on his way to church with friends. Lauren and I had just seen him a few months before, but now he didn't recognize us. The doctors told us they couldn't make any promises, it was a wait-and-see situation.

After several weeks, it was clear he was improving. Jeff had been there every day, and Ken remembered him and was responsive. The nursing staff and the neurologists had worked miracles. Ken would need several weeks of physical rehabilitation and speech therapy at a nursing center, but he would recover. He'd be fine.

Jeff was there at the hospital when he was discharged on a Friday night, and like any good big brother he gave Ken some good-natured ribbing, made a few off-color comments, and snapped a picture of Ken laughing before he was lifted into the transport vehicle. Jeff would be back to visit him in the morning, and Lauren and I were planning to drive back to Dover that day also.

But Saturday morning Jeff called. Ken had fallen while he was in the nursing center, and he was back in the emergency room.

"How?! How could he have fallen?" I yelped, and Jeff could only say, "I don't know. I just got the call. I'm going there now."

This time was different. Ken was in a coma and on a respirator, and the doctors tried to explain the difference between brain death and a vegetative state. I didn't understand the difference; I don't think any of us did. All we knew was that our brother couldn't breathe on his own, and he was hooked up to a machine and being fed through a tube.

When we found out the whole story of what happened at the nursing center, we were heartbroken, devastated, and furious. His discharge notes from the neurologist were unequivocal. He was not to be left unattended. He must have an alarm on his bed in case he tries to get up. If Ken complained of a headache, bring him back to the ER immediately. If he had any blood coming from his stitches, bring him to the ER. If he had any kind of fluid coming from his ear, bring him back to the ER. There was no gray area in this.

So when Ken complained of a headache, the nurse gave him an aspirin and walked away. When the nurse saw fresh blood on his bandage and fluid coming from his ear, she wiped it off and threw the cotton ball in the trash. And when Ken got up in the middle of the night, disoriented and confused, he fell and hit his head on the oxygen tank. Nobody came running, because his bed was not alarmed. He lay there, not breathing, for nobody knows how long, because nobody's recollection ever seemed to line up to any semblance of the truth.

Finally, a custodian mopping the hallway noticed Ken on the floor and called the nurse. She asked for a crash cart to give him oxygen, but nobody could find it. She borrowed one from another floor, but Ken still couldn't get oxygen because the cart wasn't stocked properly.

At least someone had called an ambulance; Ken only got air into his lungs when the paramedics arrived.

As Ken lay in the hospital, our mom was wondering why he didn't come visit. By now, she was in hospice care. We were afraid to tell her the truth, that he was between life and death and we didn't know if he'd recover. It was impossible for her to visit him, so we made excuses. He has a cold. He missed the bus. He had a doctor's appointment. Finally, we had to tell her the truth: he was in the hospital, but we tried to play down the seriousness.

It's a hell of a thing, having to think about who might die first. Our mom had already buried one child—our brother Steve—and we wanted to spare her the thought that we might lose Ken too. We clung to the thinnest shred of hope that we might not have to come to the worst decision anyone has to make—to keep him on life support or let him go. He might recover, right? But in our hearts, we knew. Jeff, Lauren, and I were in total agreement, we had to let him go. That was the right thing to do.

Two months to the day after Ken passed away, our mom died in her sleep. We hadn't been able to keep it from her. One day, during a visit, she just said it out of the blue. "He's dead, isn't he?" *Yes, Mom, we're sorry. He's gone.*

She nodded and said, "Thank you for not telling me before."

I wasn't the same when I came back to work. I still loved my job, and I still sculpted. But I was going in slow motion. I'd look out the window at the deer and the birds and wish I could be out there with them, not in a room full of skulls. I didn't need any more reminders of death.

15

And the Horse You Rode In On

When my lawyer called, I expected it to be notification of my court date with the EEO judge. Instead, she had news.

"Let me explain this before you get upset," she said. "The EEO is over. The FBI had submitted a petition for summary judgment in their favor, and of course we countered that. So even though you had the right to a hearing, the judge denied it by ruling instead."

There was good news and bad news. It was a split judgment. I definitively proved discrimination when the judge decreed: "I find that the Agency subjected Complainant to *unlawful discrimination* by its commission of a per se violation of Title VII, when Franklin M. Hart, Jr. told the Complainant, Lisa Bailey, 'Call off the lawyers, you don't get to call EEO, that's my decision.'"

But, out of the other side of her mouth, the judge ruled in favor of the FBI overall, stating: "I find the Complainant was not subjected to unlawful harassment on the basis of race or sex, or in reprisal for her prior involvement in EEO activity."

Say that again? How'd this happen?

Here's how: supervisors never lie. Whatever they say in their sworn statement is automatically accepted as the truth, whereas anything the employee says is a lie. I had five sworn statements from my coworkers and stacks of documentation to prove otherwise, but the judge apparently wasn't interested in seeing any of that.

My attorney also pointed out another potential reason: just as some lawyers prefer plea deals over arguing a case in court, some administrative judges don't like to bother with hearings. They'd rather make a ruling instead, clear off their desk faster, and if the employee doesn't like it, they can file an appeal. Which starts the timeline over again.

I tried to keep my temper in check while reading statements rationalizing Harry's behavior: "Mr. Dunne admitted to raising his voice and using verbal and non-verbal gestures [but] there is no corroborating evidence to support a finding that any of Mr. Dunne's yelling or gesticulating could be deemed threatening." And "Mr. Dunne's unprofessional approach was not motivated by unlawful animus on the basis of Ms. Bailey's race or sex. Mr. Dunne's actions had been motivated by self-preservation."

My lawyer was dumbfounded, saying that in her entire career she had never seen anything like it. I could appeal, but she didn't recommend it. The whole process would just start all over again taking several more years of my life, and the next judge would either rubber-stamp this decision, or worse: rule against me entirely.

The judge's ruling added that the FBI "shall consider" taking disciplinary action against Frank. The FBI considered that for about five seconds and went, *Nope, we're good here.* Frank walked away from it all, not so much as a blip on his personnel record.

The one thing that I know must have infuriated him was that he hadn't beaten me. I had proved discrimination, and the whole FBI Laboratory was going to know about it. An official notice had to be posted for ninety consecutive days in "conspicuous locations" throughout the building stating that: "Unlawful discrimination occurred at the United States Department of Justice, Federal Bureau of Investigation, Laboratory Division, Photo Unit, Quantico, Virginia."

It was in every break room on every floor, and I smiled every time I saw it. It was over. It only took tens of thousands of dollars, six years of my life, and countless refills of Xanax, but I did it. Actually, it was $83,549, but who's counting?

If your eyes just bugged out at the number, let me make this abundantly clear: no, Reid and I most certainly did not have that kind of money. Bit by bit, it went on our credit cards as the FBI lawyers filed motion after motion that my lawyer had to respond to, milking us dry. That's one of their tactics. Bankrupt the person, and they'll give up. But I didn't.

Now, all I had to do was make it through the OPR. After that, it would be smooth sailing.

———

In an OPR, the division will write a letter to investigators about the work history, professionalism, and character of the person under investigation. Depending on who is behind the OPR, the letter can go one of two ways.

If the division likes the person, they will write a glowing letter. This was evidenced by the round-up reports that the OPR office emailed employees every quarter. Everybody looked forward to them, because even though the identifying information was redacted, they made for some very juicy reading. Supervisors caught having sex in the stairwell! Agents using the database to look up dirt on their neighbor! Swiping drugs from the evidence room and getting high at work!

There would be situations where, I kid you not, an agent would get drunk, crash their bureau-owned vehicle into a tree, show their FBI badge to the police to try to talk their way out of it, and then throw up in the holding cell. But all they would get is a slap on the wrist, because the division raved about what a nice guy he was, that this was so totally out of character, and that he promises he will never do it again.

But when the division is using an OPR as a vehicle to demolish a person, they lie their asses off:

> Ms. Bailey has not accepted responsibility for her actions and poor judgement, and it is not known as to whether she has truly experienced remorse. She has great difficulty accepting that she might be wrong in thoughts or actions, and can exhibit an arrogant, self-important, and belligerent attitude.
>
> Ms. Bailey's propensity to disregard directives and instructions from even the highest levels of management within the bureau with which she disagrees demonstrates her conduct as an employee. She is difficult to manage, and her unprofessional behavior is detrimental to the morale of division personnel thereby creating an unpleasant and disruptive work environment.
>
> While talented, she is also very good at twisting the words of others, especially those who have authority over her, to her own benefit. She is notorious for hearing what she wants to hear when given specific direction, and later claiming the direction was either inadequate or lacked clarity. Her behavior often led to counseling sessions during which she typically resorted to mincing the words of others, circular logic, verbal semantics, exaggerated rationalizations, nonverbal displays of discontent, and overly literal interpretations to argue she was right. Ms. Bailey is extremely difficult to manage because of her negative unprofessional traits and or tendencies.
>
> As a result, Ms. Bailey's ability to be rehabilitated is questionable.

There was more, loads more, and I was shell-shocked. This letter would determine my punishment, and going by what it said, the OPR

AND THE HORSE YOU RODE IN ON

office would wonder why, if I was such a reprehensible employee, I hadn't been fired years before.

I was forced to read this pack of lies while sitting in Mr. Norton's conference room. I could not consult a lawyer, and I was not allowed to have a copy to refer to in my appeal. My phone was taken away so I couldn't take photographs of it. My only option was to take copious notes and try to counter every false allegation, hoping I wouldn't accidentally leave something out.

At one point while I was reading, Mr. Norton walked in. I was near tears now, part righteous anger, part desperation. This hit piece was going to do me in, and there wasn't one iota of truth to any of it. Norton appeared sympathetic.

"Mr. Norton, did you *read* this?" His signature was on it, but I had to ask.

It took him a minute to say anything. "Well, yes."

"And you *believe* this about me?"

He didn't look me in the eye, or speak. His throat just made that *ack-ack* sound that cats do when they see a fly in the window.

"Mr. Norton, you know I'm a good employee! You know none of this is true. You've seen the letters of appreciation from other agencies. I've got tons of letters from agents thanking me, even letters from Dr. Bunsen congratulating me on my good work. You've thanked me yourself! I mean, I was even nominated for the Director's Award."

His eyes grew wide with surprise. "How do you know about that?" he said quickly.

"The legat told me. He emailed me when he submitted my nomination last year."

The FBI Director's Award for Excellence is the absolute highest honor the FBI bestows, and the Bogotá team was just announced as the recipient.

"But I didn't see your name on the award," Norton said.

"I know. My name was taken off the list by somebody at headquarters. The legat wrote to me a few days ago apologizing, saying he didn't know it had been changed until he saw the award announcement."

Harry and Frank had always hidden compliments from agents about my work, and by Norton's reaction I wondered if he had done the same thing. Maybe he never expected that I'd ever find out. I don't know who removed my name or why, and I didn't really care. Taking away the award didn't change the experience I had there, and that's what mattered to me.

"Who wrote this?" I asked. "I mean, if I was even half of what this letter says I am, you guys would have been jeopardizing casework and the FBI's reputation to let me do *any* of the work I've done! It would have been crazy, and dangerous, to send me to Bogotá, or to interview terrorist suspects and kidnap victims, or work on any of the high-profile cases that I've worked on. Every single one of my appraisals have been 'excellent' or 'outstanding,' I've never had anything lower than that, ever."

From his silence, I had a growing, awful feeling.

It took me a minute to form the words: "Mr. Norton, did you have *Frank* write this?"

It was too awful to contemplate. Was this division that corrupt, that conniving, that devious? To have the man who had been found guilty of discrimination against me write the very document that my punishment hinged on, on fabricated charges, no less? It couldn't be true, could it?

Yes. Yes, it was.

Norton didn't look me in the eye while he feebly answered, "Well, he was your supervisor at the time, so—"

"Yes! The supervisor who was cyberstalking me, sabotaging my casework, tampering with evidence, shredding documents, and spreading lies about me!"

Until that moment, I had thought that Mr. Norton was a nice guy, and everything going on with the EEO and OPR was out of his hands. But he was as dirty as the rest.

"Why is Frank even working here anymore? Shouldn't he have been fired? The FBI says there is zero tolerance for discrimination, and he was found guilty of it. That should have meant dismissal!"

I was beyond incredulity and rage, and had been transported to a new level of fury. I had to make myself shut up, because I was afraid I might say something that would really get me in trouble. Now, I knew what Norton's ploy was: his benevolence in transferring me to the Science Unit was meant to be temporary. The problem of Lisa, who dared to point out the discrimination and reprisal that ran rampant at the bureau, would soon take care it itself courtesy of Frank's letter.

I don't remember when he walked out of the room. I was too disgusted, too furious. I pulled myself together and kept reading how awful of a person I was. The report ran eight pages long, and my hand started cramping as I copied down as much of it as I could.

When I got to the last paragraph, I had a glimmer of hope:

> There are several strong mitigating factors: you have no prior disciplinary history; you repeatedly made good faith efforts to obtain multiple approvals over a period of several months, you seem to have been generally confused about the applicable requirements, and you received conflicting advice from the Office of Integrity and Compliance, your supervisors, and Director Bunsen. Under normal circumstances your dereliction might be handled as a performance matter.

Yes! A "performance matter" meant that it wouldn't go on record as a disciplinary action. I would be in the clear. But then came the next sentence that was meant to get me fired: "However, OPR cannot ignore the division's strongly worded and extremely negative assessment of you."

The punishment for the thing I didn't do would be a letter of censure, a dismissal, or anything in between. The next several weeks were excruciating as I waited for the decision.

Would I still have a job? If my punishment was dismissal, that would be the end of my federal career. I would lose my security clearance, and any hope of ever working in forensics again. Reid and I would have to move and find some way to pay off the lawyer bills while I looked for another job. I tried not to obsess over the injustice of it all, but there was nothing I could do.

Finally, the decision came down: I would be suspended for two days. It wasn't fair, but it could have been much, much worse. I'm sure Frank was having hissy fits that his manifesto hadn't resulted in my termination, and I could at least smile at the thought.

And now I knew who the real enemy was: Norton.

If he had possessed one shred of integrity, he would have stopped the witch hunt altogether. If nothing else, he should have had Melanie write that letter. I had already gotten my first performance appraisal from her, and it was "Outstanding" across the board. "Ms. Bailey is a pleasure to work with," she wrote, "and is a wonderful addition to the unit."

I had to take the suspension in stride. File it away somewhere in the back of my brain and get over it. I turned the suspension into a four-day weekend and went shopping with Lauren.

———

Polygraphs are the FBI's get-out-of-jail-free card. When all else fails—the PIP, the OPR, or any other three-letter acronym you can think of—the FBI always has your security clearance to hold over your head.

Remember Robert Hanssen, the spy? He was a huge embarrassment to the FBI, and they could have caught him if they had followed up on any of the red flags that other employees brought up. Did you know that his own brother-in-law sounded the warning bell? He was even an agent too, but he was junior to Hanssen, the star agent with the exceptional work record and twenty years more experience. There is a hierarchy in the FBI, and even though we are duty bound to report infractions, it only goes in one direction. The shit, especially at the FBI, always rolls downhill.

After the Hanssen fallout, the FBI instituted a new policy: prospective employees must be able to pass a polygraph, but anyone who already worked at the bureau was "grandfathered" in. There are people who have worked there for thirty or forty years with access to all kinds of highly classified data, but they've never once been polygraphed.

Everyone with a top-secret clearance still has to go through a security update every five years, but it consists of an interview with an agent. Only people with the "sensitive compartmented information" designation need to keep taking the polygraph. I had that designation while in the Graphic Unit, left over from my time in the navy, but it was supposed to have been downgraded once I went to the Photo Unit. No one is ever supposed to carry more clearance than they need. But Frank refused to submit the paperwork.

"Why, Frank? Doesn't it cost the FBI a lot of money and man-hours to jump through all these hoops for a high-level clearance I don't need? I haven't ever worked on anything remotely at that level."

"That's not your concern," said Frank, "and that's final."

When I went to the Science Unit and finally had a reasonable boss again, my unit chief agreed with me. Melanie wrote to the security office at headquarters, but then *they* said no. She asked why, and was given a vague answer, like "Just in case she needs it sometime." That puzzled both of us, because it goes against FBI policy, not to mention every national security rule on the books. Especially after Hanssen. Why does a person who sculpts all day need such a sensitive clearance?

But you can't argue with headquarters. I just chalked it up to someone not wanting to deal with the paperwork.

Then, in early 2019, I got notice that my security update was in progress. No biggie, I thought. I would fill out a form, talk to an agent, and be polygraphed. I had done it four times already in my FBI career. But when I saw one of the questions on the form was about being OPR'd, I got it.

"What offense did you commit?"

My pen hovered in the air for a moment, then I made a decision. "None. I was OPR'd after filing an EEO complaint against my supervisor."

I know, I know. I probably should have bowed my head and written something like, "I did a bad, bad thing and am deeply sorry for my actions." But I couldn't do it. I had followed FBI policy to the letter and had all the documentation to prove it in case anyone was interested in the truth.

My previous polygraph had been a cakewalk. After less than forty-five minutes, I was out the door with a resounding pass. But this one? This one took three hours on a bright and sunny Thursday morning in April, and the specter of Robert Hanssen was front and center.

Was I ever unhappy with my supervisor? they asked. *That's a security red flag, you know; Hanssen didn't like his supervisors either! I might go running to the Russians or China if I didn't like my supervisor! Happens all the time! Are you in debt? Robert Hanssen was; that's why he became a spy! If you owe a lot of money, you're a prime candidate for being targeted by the enemy!*

"Yes, actually, my husband and I do owe a lot of money. Eighty thousand dollars, since you're asking. That's what it cost in lawyer's fees due to all the FBI lawyers trying to bankrupt us and force me to quit during the EEO process."

And on and on it went, and I could only keep repeating the truth: "No, I don't know any foreign agents. No, I haven't handled or even had access to any classified material in the past ten years, so it's impossible for me to access secret material, much less top secret."

The agent eyed me suspiciously as he unplugged all the wires, and then he sat across from me and sternly said, "Your results are inconclusive"—meaning, *I'm just not sure if you're telling the truth about colluding with the enemy and committing treason.* He wasn't sure about that part.

"I'll need to have another polygrapher review your chart."

Since polygraph results are subjective (otherwise, why would they need another person to review them?) and are not accepted in court (because they aren't scientific in the least), the FBI is free to make whatever judgment it wants.

Let's say you decide that you'll take another polygraph. Knowing that you're an honest person and not plotting the overthrow of the government, you're sure you're going to pass. But what if it's inconclusive again? That's it; you're toast. But you don't know it yet. You'll be sitting at your desk one day and Felicia, the human resources unit chief, will come walking down the hall with one of the armed FBI police officers, and they will turn down your corridor and open the door to your office, and that's it: they've revoked your clearance, and there's not a damn thing you can do about it. You pack up your belongings in front of your open-mouthed coworkers. You're walked out to your car. Then they follow you in an FBI police car to escort you off the base.

I took the next day off to think.

I was terrified that if I had gone in that day, security would be there to walk me out. Was I being paranoid? I might pass the next polygraph. But why was this one inconclusive in the first place?

I thought about the times I requested to be debriefed out of the extra level of security clearance. I thought about the years of abuse and humiliation, the $80,000 that Reid and I were in debt, and all the times that FBI management had lied or shirked their duty. Harry, Frank, Darla, Ms. Morningside, Dr. Bunsen, Mr. Norton, the FBI lawyers, the investigators. I didn't go through all that just to have them fail me on my polygraph, pull my clearance, and make me walk the Green Mile. I wasn't going to do it.

Earlier in the year, I had talked to Melanie about the possibility of me and Reid moving away from Virginia. He had some business opportunities in Los Angeles, and depending on how things shook out we might need to move out west. The only thing was, we wouldn't know how fast. It might be a year's notice, it might be a month.

"I will give you as much advance notice as humanly possible. If I can't give you several months, I promise it will be two weeks."

I was not the same person that I was when I had started. I used to believe in the FBI implicitly, and now I didn't. When I knew in my bones that I would never be able to trust anything FBI management told me, I knew I was done.

I emailed Melanie and told her I was giving my notice. She called soon after, worried and upset, and asking what happened. I'm pretty sure I cried, because I loved working for her and I loved my job, but I just couldn't do it anymore. I thought the years of worrying were over, but it never would be. It would never stop.

She called me later in the day and said she had talked to head-quarters, and they had assured her that nothing would happen until I took the next polygraph. I trusted Melanie, and I trusted that she had called them.

But I came in on the weekend to finish up my cases and pack my personal items, just in case. If headquarters had lied to Melanie, and I ended up getting walked out after all, I'd at least be able to leave with just my purse, and some shred of dignity.

I came to work Monday and tried to act all nonchalant, like, *Of course I'd never leave without saying goodbye*, but yes, it was true; I was retiring. Two weeks' notice, exactly.

When I was waiting all those years ago to get a start date for the FBI, the movie *Miss Congeniality* came out. Sandra Bullock played an FBI agent who goes undercover in a beauty pageant. It's a really cute movie, and Lauren and I saw it countless times.

William Shatner plays the pageant emcee and asks the sweet-but-not-too-bright Miss Rhode Island what her idea of a perfect date would be. Instead of describing a romantic walk on the beach or dinner with her boyfriend, she names a specific date on the calendar.

I had to give the Human Resources Unit a specific date on the calendar, too, as my official last day of work, so I counted two weeks forward from that awful polygraph and laughed when I realized my career had come full circle.

I retired on the very same day Miss Rhode Island had chosen, and it was perfect: "April 25. Because it's not too hot, not too cold. All you need is a light jacket."

It's unsettling how many federal employees start counting down the days to retirement when it's decades away. Some start the clock on their first day of work, and those were the kind of people I never wanted to work with. The feeling was mutual; they mocked anyone who actually enjoyed their work and gave it their all.

The FBI likes to prepare employees for the day they retire and gives us a timeline for the process. Not so much for the employees' sake, as for its own. There are thirty-five thousand people in the bureau, and there are multiple offices involved with out-processing a person. There's the human resources office, payroll, health insurance, life insurance, pension, security—it gets quite involved. The timeline starts one year out from the anticipated retirement date and goes from there: talk to an accountant a year ahead of time, at six months notify this office, at three months send us this form, and so on.

As you go to retirement seminars and start sending in all the paperwork to the various offices in headquarters, word begins to spread. Everyone knows when somebody is a year or less away from retiring because it's like getting sprung from prison.

The employee is excitedly talking about all the free time they're going to have, and it's a fun game to play with your pals when you bump into them in the hallway: "Three more months, baby. I'll think of you when I'm drinking a margarita on the beach!"

It's not just logistics that are important. This yearlong timeline is also good for the employee to have time to mentally prepare, because retirement can be a shock to the system, especially if you're a person who loves her job like I did.

I had it all planned out: I was going to retire in June 2021, when I turned sixty. At first, I'd just relax. I'd start doing some of my own artwork. I didn't know exactly what that would be, but I figured it would reveal itself to me when the time came. I might get a part-time job until Reid retired, and then we'd move to Europe and explore the world.

But suddenly, I was free. It was overwhelming and exhilarating, and my brain couldn't process it. I hadn't had time to digest the reality of it. The one thing that was foremost in my mind was that I hadn't given the FBI the satisfaction of taking away my clearance. I hadn't been sacked, and I hadn't been escorted off base. I dropped the mic and strode out the building with my head held high, and it felt awesome.

The night that Reid and I decided I would put in my notice, we had come to another decision: we were going to move to Vegas so he would be close to Los Angeles for the project he was working on. We wanted to start fresh somewhere else, getting as far away from Washington, DC, the FBI, and two-hour commutes as possible. We just needed to wait for the end of our lease, so I had four months' free time.

True to form, I stayed busy. I organized our apartment to within an inch of its life. I packed, made trips to Goodwill, put things up for sale on eBay. I visited my cousins, went antiquing with Lauren, read books and watched movies, and stayed up as late as I wanted.

I swore that I wasn't about to let myself waste one more second of my life thinking about Harry or Frank, the FBI, and the injustice I had been through. I compartmentalized it and filed it all away just like the other unpleasant things I had seen on the job—mountains of pain and gore—and it worked.

One night, I woke up at 3:00 AM and couldn't get back to sleep, so I tried my foolproof remedy: hot chocolate and an old Bette Davis movie. And I was back asleep in ten minutes.

But the next night I woke up at 3:00 AM again. And then the next night, and the next, and the next, and no amount of hot chocolate could calm me down. I was waking up shaking, furious, and full of impotent rage, my thoughts racing. Everything I had pushed down and vowed to forget was escaping back to the surface. I went to the computer and started writing it all down, just a free flow of words as it all spilled from my brain. When I couldn't type fast enough to keep up, I'd talk into my iPhone and paste it in later.

For weeks, I'd go to bed at 11:00 PM, wake up at 3:00 AM, and write until the afternoon. I should have been exhausted, but adrenaline kept me going. There was still so much more that I wanted to do with forensic art. I still loved it all, and they had done their best to ruin me, to attack me where it mattered most: my expertise.

As the words poured out and the pages piled up, that righteous fury and anger gave way to a sort of incredulous hilarity—like, *Can you believe what these guys did? Seriously?* It was crazy. The whole hideous nightmare was so over the top, so blatant, so outrageous, so asinine, so ridiculous. Who would ever believe that it could ever happen, especially in the FBI?

Once I started laughing, I couldn't stop. Harry and Frank were not men. They were two angry little boys who knew they could bully me as much as they wanted and get away with it because they had the FBI protecting them, a daddy to hold their hands, kiss them on their little foreheads, and make all the bad stuff go away.

When the Harvey Weinstein article came out in the *New York Times*, I remember thinking, *This is going to be huge.* He wasn't a household name in 2017, but I already knew exactly who he was, because Lauren and I were devoted watchers of the Oscar ceremony every year, and every year one actress or another would tearfully thank Harvey while the camera panned to an oafish-looking man stuffed into an expensive tuxedo with a face like half-chewed bubble gum.

I shuddered when I read the articles, and as more and more women spoke up, I realized that the tactics the FBI had used to silence me were taken right from Harvey's playbook. When I pulled myself together and looked at what I had written, I realized I wasn't just blowing off steam anymore. I needed to speak up. I certainly don't expect the FBI to change, but I had to let other women know what happened to me so they could protect themselves.

There's a terrific quote from Catherine Aird, the English crime novelist, that perfectly sums it up: "If you can't be a good example, then you'll just have to be a horrible warning."

––––––––––

Do I hate the FBI? I should, shouldn't I?

But I can't; there are too many amazing people there, those I've worked with and those I never had the opportunity to. They are some of the most qualified, brilliant, tenacious, dedicated people I have ever had the honor of working with, and they take the job seriously. They mean it when they say they are fighting for justice. And they mean it when they say they are working on behalf of victims. It's not an act. It's real.

However, I do hate the part of the FBI that not only allowed this to happen but encouraged it, threw gasoline on it, and then covered up the ashes. I hold every level of management there accountable: whoever was involved, whoever knew about it and said nothing, all the way up to the director's office, whoever was sitting in that chair when everything went down, and whoever may be sitting there now, even if he (or maybe she?) wasn't there at the time.

As the leader of an agency with "investigation" as part of its name, how can any director possibly think that a spotless EEO record in an organization of over thirty-five thousand people is legit? That it was earned? It wasn't, and you know it—and if you don't, you damn well should have the curiosity of mind to wonder, *Are we still the good guys?*

But I'm done now. I'm done with thinking about what I went through, about the FBI, about the injustice. I gave it more hours out of my life than I ever should have had to, and I don't owe one second more.

I'm done with death too. I've done my part, and all I want to do now is focus on life. Of course, I'll never be able to look at a skull and not start putting a face on it in my head. I can't help it; it's part of my DNA now. I don't keep track of my facial approximations either. Whenever I happen to find out that another has been identified, I'm torn. Of course, one part of me is pleased, but the other part knows that a family has gotten awful news.

There's no need, or even desire on my part, to get back into forensic art. I will always keep helping aspiring artists and give them as much advice and encouragement as I possibly can. I tell them the reality of the job, how hard it is to get your foot in the door, and how hard it is to stay there. I loved forensic art with every fiber of my being, but it's their turn now. And I hope they end up loving it as much as I did.

As "luck" would have it, Covid hit a few months after Reid and I moved to Vegas. After a year of watching our life pass by in a two-bedroom apartment, we fast-tracked our dream of moving to Europe. We landed in Portugal, and it's like living in a travel show. Mere blocks from the river, seagulls flying past our window, two-hour lunches, and the loveliest people I have ever met.

For years, the most intimidating thing in the world for me was a blank sheet of paper. But now, I've got sketchbooks with hundreds of pages to fill, and I'm not scared one bit. I draw whatever I want, whenever I want, and it's overwhelming and freeing and wonderful.

It's a magical world. And it's time for me and Reid to go exploring.

ACKNOWLEDGMENTS

I would be totally lost in this world without my amazing husband and best friend, Reid. You keep me sane and make me laugh, and I'm so grateful for every second that we have together. I know everything the FBI did affected you as deeply as it did me, and even more so on some levels. We made it out stronger than ever. I love the life we've made together and love you more than I can ever express.

I am so thankful for my family. My sweet, wonderful, warm, hilarious dad, Walter Edgar Brown Jr., who is still a constant presence in my life. My mom, Carolyn Brown, for inspiring me as an artist; I wish you knew how good you really were. My oldest brother Jeff, family historian and Wordle wizard, always in search of the next big story. Ken, the kindest soul, stealthy card sharp, master of bad jokes and ridiculous puns. You were too good for this world. And Steve, the epitome of marine discipline, excellence, and pride, with the wicked sense of humor and nerves of steel. I still have dreams where you've been on a secret deployment this whole time and wake up thinking you're here.

And Lauren, my "bestest pal" in the whole wide world, who also happens to be my big sister. Who else knows the entire history of my life? Who else will talk for hours about topics we've beaten to death a thousand times over, who knows me inside and out, makes me laugh until I can't breathe, speaks in code using 1940s movie quotes, happily hangs out with me doing absolutely nothing, and talks on the phone while we're each driving to meet up because it takes an hour to get to the mall and we don't want to waste any time? "Gimme a kidney? It's yours!"

And my cousin Diane, who would still be a best friend even if we weren't related. Thanks for reading the early version of this book and offering wisecracks and wisdom, along with a nice glass of merlot. Aunt Mona and Uncle Buddy must be looking down and smiling.

I was beyond thrilled and busting with pride the day that Jessica Papin agreed to be my literary agent, and that feeling hasn't diminished one bit. Thank you for always having my back and believing that this was a story worth telling.

Thank you to Jerome Pohlen and the wonderful team at Chicago Review Press for taking this book on and being so good at what you do. Also, thank you for your infinite patience as the wheels of the FBI review process ground on, and on, and on.

Special accolades to Danny Freedman. Your guidance and encouragement were a lifeline to me. You challenged me to dig into areas that I hadn't thought of and made me into a better writer.

A heartfelt thank you to Kathryn Cray, quite possibly the wisest woman on the planet, who helped me navigate those hellish years at work. You always know just what to say, and you're always right.

Thank you to Jeni Fairey, who made me into a better sculptor in a matter of days. I hope to visit again for more talking and laughing over wine and chocolate.

A great big group hug and deep thanks to my second family, the Graphic Unit at Johns Hopkins, for the best working experience of my life: Dan Brocklebank, Don Vislay, Robin Walker, Kevin McCafferty, Cathy Peacock, and Ian Williamson. I was so thrilled to become an artist there and really hit the lottery being part of the group. I looked forward to going to work every morning because of you.

And there aren't enough superlatives to express how much I adore Barbara Williamson, the absolute best boss in the world who made it all possible, and who happens to be an amazingly heroic woman to boot. You always had our backs, and never stopped championing us. You are a force of nature, and woe be unto anyone who messes with someone you love. I'm an artist because of you.

Special appreciation goes to the man in charge, Dan Tyler, who made such a wonderful work environment at Hopkins possible. I don't know of any other person who could be "one of the gang" while commanding respect and running an entire department to boot. The FBI could learn a few things from you about leadership.

Thank you, Adria Zeldin, my tenacious lawyer who took on the good fight with the FBI. I never would have stood a chance without you.

I absolutely loved being a forensic artist, and much of that is due to the amazing people I met along the way:

Chuck Jackson, an all-out hilarious person and trusted friend. I admire you so much. You epitomize everything that is good and right in the field of forensic art.

Wes Neville, who went through his own amount of hell in the Photo Unit. From day one at the FBI, you were an open book, sharing everything you knew about facial approximation and sculpting with me. That's such a rare thing in the field nowadays. Thank you for the friendship, teamwork, and hours and hours and hours of talking about skulls.

Jim Brennan, a virtual encyclopedia of all things FBI, and one of the kindest, most genuine people I have ever met. Bob Thomas, who is meticulous as hell and proud of it. Jeff Bell, an exacting photographer with the soul of an artist.

Mike Streed, a forensic art rebel in the best way, who is always looking for innovative ways to make the field better, and truly works on the side of the victim.

Liz Weening, a longtime trusted friend who did what others only talk about. Not just working as a forensic artist but identifying a victim as a result. I'm in awe.

Gene O'Donnell, I am truly thankful for your mentorship in forensic art, and your support of the VICTIMS and Body Farm projects. I wish you hadn't retired when you did.

In addition to the research at the Body Farm project, a huge part of my time at the FBI was working to create a national database for unidentified remains: the VICTIMS Project. It was also my biggest heartbreak. Politics and money ended up taking precedence over the unidentified, and VICTIMS was cancelled. Still, there were people who poured their heart and soul into the project, and they deserve recognition for their truly valiant efforts:

Melissa Torpey, I'm so grateful that you were part of the team. I admire you so much, and will never forget your speech at the AAFS, which was brave as hell. What can I say? The FBI blew it when they lost you.

And the late Phil Williams, my deep appreciation for your work on VICTIMS. Thank you for trying to make it happen, but I guess it was doomed from the start.

I truly appreciate the kindness shown to me by everyone in the "Science Unit," who had an artist unexpectedly dropped in their laps one day. Now you know how it came about, and why I kept saying I was so happy to be there.

ABOUT THE AUTHOR

Lisa Bailey is a retired FBI forensic artist, adjunct faculty member of the FBI Academy, and instructor of the FBI Forensic Facial Imaging Class. She has been featured prominently in major news outlets such as the *Washington Post*, NPR, *America's Most Wanted*, *Dateline NBC*, and *A&E Real Crime*. Bailey and her forensic art also appear in *Mental Floss*, Medium, the Smithsonian, and the National Museum of Health and Medicine. Visit her online at lisabaileyauthor.com.